STOCK CAR RACING U.S.A.

---------------------------→

STOCK CAR

RACING U.S.A.

Produced by Lyle Kenyon Engel

Text by Jim Hunter
Edited by George Engel and Marla Ray

DODD, MEAD & COMPANY · NEW YORK

INTRODUCTION BY RICHARD PETTY

——————————————————————————➤

Stock car racing is my life and it has been since I was twelve years old. That might be a little bit too strong a statement—but not all that much. My introduction came when my daddy, Lee Petty, first decided that racing was a good way to make a living. And his entry into the sport came just about the same time that a bunch of racers got together and formed the association that is known as the National Association for Stock Car Auto Racing (NASCAR).

Maybe the best place to start would be with the sport before NASCAR got started. You will hear a lot about the early days being just a Sunday get-together among the boys who were running liquor in their souped-up cars. Quite a bit of it's true, but quite a bit of it's legend. No matter how it started, it was a bunch of people who liked fast cars enough to go to the trouble of putting them together and running them in competition.

It didn't take too long before some promoters got the idea that this would be a good show. So they organized the races in empty fields and pastures and charged admission. The only trouble was that there were often two races in different directions. The drivers themselves would fight it out for the checkered flag and the promoter would be heading as fast as he could in a different direction with the money he had promised as a purse for the winner. You can rest assured that the boys drove just as fast after the promoter as they did after each other.

That was pretty much the way things were until 1948 when a group of racers in Daytona Beach got together and worked out the details of what we know as NASCAR. They were pioneers—Bill France, Joe Littlejohn, Red Vogt, Alvin Hawkins, Sam Packard, Tom Gallen, Frank Mundy, Bob Osiecki, Harvey Tattersall, Bob Richards, Bill Streeter, Marshall Teague, Bill Tuthill and Buddy Shuman.

One of the first things this group did was to come up with the concept of stock car racing. They decided to hold a race in Charlotte that would feature only stock cars—the kind of cars that you could buy in the showrooms; and they were going to run them stock—without any of the tricks that they had in the modifieds that had run earlier. With that decision, they laid the foundations for what has become one of the most popular forms of racing in the history of the sport.

Daddy just couldn't be left out. He and my Uncle Julie borrowed a 1948 Buick from a friend and decided to run it in the race. Daddy was doing pretty well until he broke a sway bar and flipped the car four times. He got out without being hurt, but he had some tall explaining to do to his friend.

That's how it started for us and we've been in it ever since. Everybody was learning in those days. A lot of the running was done on horse racetracks—it was all dirt track stuff—and the suspensions began breaking and causing wrecks. So, with safety at stake, the NASCAR inspector began looking the other way when the boys began using heavy-duty shocks and springs—and it was just a matter of time until we got heavy-duty wheels, hubs, spindles and all the rest of the suspension pieces.

Pretty soon the stock cars were becoming race cars that looked like passenger cars. In those days we were really proud of what we were doing, even though it was primitive by today's standards. As NASCAR grew in popularity, new tracks were built and new interest came from different areas and the sport progressed by leaps and bounds. In the early days the biggest thing that happened was 1¼ of the meanest miles of asphalt that has ever been laid—Darlington. That name had magic then and it still does—it's the granddaddy of them all.

When we showed up at Darlington, South Carolina, for the first annual running of the Labor Day race in 1950 no one was really prepared for what was coming up. The track was faster than anything we had ever seen. It was banked in the first and second turns and flat in three and four and it took a special technique at each corner. Cars couldn't drive two abreast through three and four and it was demanding on cars and drivers.

Most of the hot dogs were there in big, powerful cars. Daddy and a fellow named Johnny Mantz both were driving Plymouths, which were lighter and plenty strong. They gave away a little speed on the straights, but they more than made it up in the corners. And one important thing—because they were lighter, they were easier on tires. Those big, heavy cars went through tires like popcorn and Daddy and Mantz just chugged along and were in the lead a good deal of the time.

Mantz made two contributions to the sport that day. He introduced racing tires, which he had picked up in Akron, and he recorded the first modern pit stop. When he came in to change tires and get gas, his crew had pneumatic tools that removed the lug nuts in record time. That gave him a real edge on the field and he ended up winning the first annual Southern 500 with a speed of 76 miles an hour.

Up until the early 1950s, the only changes the racers were making to the cars were in the suspensions. About that time, they started working on the engines, polishing the parts and generally working to get more power. This is where the real skills started showing. Racing's no big mystery. The people who work the hardest are the ones who are going to do the best week after week. If everyone on the circuit had the same equipment and the same amount of money available to them, you'd find that the same ones would be winning that are winning now. Back in the early Fifties, what the good, hardworking mechanics were doing one year, everyone would be doing the next.

In the mid-Fifties things really got rolling and stock car racing was headed for the big time—the factories discovered the sport. For years people had just naturally rooted for one make against the other. I remember when Daddy was driving Dodges and Plymouths, people would come up to him and say, "Lee, how come you let that Hudson beat you," or "I bet my cousin $10 that your Plymouth was faster than the Oldsmobile." So it was just natural for Detroit to capitalize on this built-in loyalty.

Actually, most of the makes were winners, at one time or another. Oldsmobiles were tough and earned a lot of wins at one time; Hudsons were the hot tip for a while, Plymouths and Dodges —where we specialized—were fast, durable and a little lighter than the others. Then came the Chrysler with the 331-cubic-inch engine. Daddy won his first championship in one of those.

When the factories came on the scene they brought something to the sport that hadn't been there before—a high level of technology and money to prepare the best cars. The battle lines were quickly drawn among the Big Three and they really raced in earnest until pressure from Washington against speed and horsepower cut the race short. That era was when Ford and General Motors really got to locking horns. First Ford came out with a 312-cubic-inch supercharged engine and Chevy followed with a fuel-injected V8. Then Oldsmobile came out with a 371-cubic-inch engine. That's the way things were until the factories pulled out, and many think those were the golden days.

It was in 1958 that I first drove. It wasn't dramatic—Daddy had asked me to wait until I was twenty-one before I drove and shortly after my twenty-first birthday I told him I wanted to give it a try. He pointed to a year-old Oldsmobile that he had run and said, "Get that car ready." My cousin, Dale Inman, and I began working on the car and pretty soon we were racing. I finished sixth in my first race on the old convertible circuit and began the long learning process. I'm not going to spend a lot of time on my driving career. I just want to tell about how all this happened and how it got to where it is today.

Daytona was to the 1960s what Darlington was to the 1950s. It was big, fast and modern. At 2½ miles, it was by far the biggest track any of us had ever run on. The first race there was actually in 1959, but it was the story of the times during the decade of the 1960s. The following year superspeedways were opened at Charlotte and Atlanta, and then in 1965 came the tough mile-long track at Rockingham, North Carolina. Those four tracks, plus Darlington, still comprise the Grand Slam of stock car racing, and believe me, it takes some fancy running to pull off victories at each of them.

I was lucky. By the time Daytona was having its first race, I was just beginning my driving career. I hadn't developed a bunch of habits on the shorter tracks as many of the drivers had and I didn't have to unlearn a whole lot. If you had to pick a time to start racing Grand National stock cars, that was it. The tracks were just as new to the veteran drivers as they were to me and we all learned together. Daddy won the first race ever run at the Daytona Speedway in a three-way photo finish that took three days of studying the photographs to call.

At the start of the 1960s the factories were for all intents and purposes out of racing. We all worked hard and had good times. Then, as the crowds grew and the sport began growing in recognition, the factories started sneaking back into the sport. Pontiac was the first and then came Chevrolet and pretty soon all the rest of them were back in. Ford made its big plunge in 1963 and Chrysler came back in earnest in 1964 when they unveiled the Hemi engine

9

at Daytona. And that one moment ushered in the mid-1960s, which gave birth to some of the finest automobile racing of any kind that has ever been seen.

By 1964 GM was all but out—there were some leftover bits and pieces that some of the boys ran, but nothing really serious as far as a winning effort was concerned. It was Ford and Chrysler and Chrysler and Ford. In 1965 the Hemi was outlawed just because it was faster than anything else. We came back in 1966 and won the early races so decisively that Ford quit for most of the season. By 1967 we all were racing again and we ran that way in one form or another until 1971, when Ford dropped out. By 1972 Chrysler also ended its support program and there we were back where it started.

But things were different again—they're never the same. For one thing, there were more supertracks—new facilities at Talladega, Alabama, Bryan, Texas, Irish Hills, Michigan, and Ontario, California. Purses were bigger than ever and racing still was good. Cars had changed from stock models with minor modifications to full-fledged race cars at about $20,000 a copy. Speeds on the major tracks approach the 200-mile-an-hour mark.

In the nearly twenty-five years that NASCAR has been in operation a lot has happened. There have been good races and bad races; we've been friends with everyone and we've been at each other's throats; we don't always agree and sometimes our disagreements make a lot more noise than our agreements. But through it all we have been together. If you want to put it one way, it's like a family. You don't always agree with each other, but you are a family.

Like I said, I wasn't planning to talk a lot about the people and places here—I just wanted to tell how we got where we are. You can find out most of the other stuff in this book. It's a good one.

CONTENTS

PREFACE

———————————————————————→

He knew it was bad. The trail was too easy to follow. Puddles of blood stained the polished corridor that led from the hospital emergency entrance to the closed door. In the hallway, still wearing a soft blue dress that minutes before had emphasized her striking features, Elizabeth Petty was pale with fear. She prayed, and a writer remarked, "There's a blue angel if ever I've seen one." Her son, Richard, went right into the room where his father lay gravely injured. Richard Petty knew his father was hurt; the telltale corridor trail left no doubts in the young race driver's mind.

Just a few minutes before, Lee Petty had been speeding around Daytona International Speedway like blue blazes, battling for the lead in a Grand National stock car race. Now, Lee Petty's battle was for life, against the clock of all time. His Plymouth stock car had soared over the four-story guard rail with Johnny Beauchamp's machine tied to its metal. The two cars crashed to the ground far below with the force of Beauchamp's car leaving Petty a bundle of broken bones. His car was a bundle of ready-made scrap iron.

Doctors didn't figure Lee Petty would make it through the night as he desperately clung to life with the same strength and spirit so many had come to admire behind speeding wheels. Richard Petty leaned over the bed to hear a whispering voice say, "Son, you take Momma on home and get the race cars fixed up. I'll be all right. I'll come on home in a couple of days." Richard Petty's daddy had always taught him, "Son, you've got to take the good with the bad in this business." That day, for perhaps the first time, Lee Petty's son knew what he had always meant. Stock car racing is no sport for sissies. Nor will it likely ever be.

The very nature of a sport that had its beginnings on mountain back roads better known to bottleggers than bears kept it from drawing its most ardent pupils from dignified city life. When NASCAR, the National Association for Stock Car Auto Racing, was organized in 1948, it sought to bring order and respect to a struggling sport most people regarded in much the same way as a human cannonball at a county fair. They thought the people racing stock cars around and around the dusty, rutty fairgrounds tracks were just plain crazy, or just plain hungry.

For the most part they were just plain crazy, because, prior to NASCAR's formation, drivers racing for tidbits of prize money had no more assurance they would collect than Uncle Sam had of collecting on illegal liquor at the time. Those staging the barnyard scrambles were not always blessed with integrity. The self-styled code adopted by most race organizers at the time was similar to the honor normally reserved among thieves: Promise whatever it takes to stage a race, then light out with the cashbox.

Stock car racing promoters of the late Forties and early Fifties did just that. More than one of NASCAR's regular competitors today remember those days which carried over into NASCAR's fledgling years. "Guys back in those days liked to fight just as much as they liked to race," says Alf Knight, who watched stock car racing take on white pants and fancy shoes after discarding coveralls and brogans. "I remember lots of times when the best stock car drivers never won. Lots of the best drivers couldn't fight a lick, but they knew they would have had to after a race to prove they had won it. Instead, they'd just settle for a spot back in the field in front of some other guy they knew wouldn't be interested in fighting. Lots of times, they'd have to drop back pretty far to find one."

Boys back in 1949 and 1950 spent as much time courting cars as girls. Shiny chrome and fender skirts seemed just as important as silly girls swirling around in saddle oxfords and bobby sox. And just as sexy.

"Not a whole lot of boys had time to mess around playing football and that kind of stuff in the rural areas back in those days," says Barney Wallace, current president of Darlington International Raceway. "Lots of them had to go to school and then tend to chores on the farm. About the only time they had any free time at all was Saturday. That's how lots of them got started with racing stock cars. Just about every little town had some form of race track. It was usually a pasture that wasn't being used. Or an old horse track that had outlived its days.

"They'd have a stock car race about once a month, and boys would get together and build themselves a car. They'd race it just to attract some pretty little girl's attention. More times than not, the toughest boy in the crowd would wind up driving it. Earn the seat, so to speak. It was great fun watching. They'd knock each other all over the place. More often than not the cars wouldn't have any fenders on them once they finished racing. So, pretty soon, they just started fixing them without the fenders to start with."

It was wild: Fords, Chevies, Plymouths, DeSotos, Pontiacs, Buicks, Dodges, Cadillacs, Hudsons, Henry-Js, Nashes—you name it, somebody raced it. The local folks loved it. Coveralled cowboys riding roughshod over race courses unfit for walking, much less driving.

"I remember one of the biggest injuries drivers used to suffer was knots on their heads," says Ernie Moore, another veteran race official who remembers the head-cracking beginnings of the sport so crude in its nature neighborhood preachers denounced it as totally unholy, among other things.

"I remember this one old boy at a race down in south Georgia one time knocked himself out five times in one race," says Moore. "It was supposed to be a fifteen-lap feature around an old cornfield. They had just chopped the stalks and the rows were still visible. One of the corners got real bad. They was a hole there about five feet deep. The cars would hit that hole and the drivers' heads would bang against the roof of the car. They'd hang outta those old cars when they hit that hole. That one old boy knocked himself cuckoo five times. And every time, he crashed into another car. Nobody had racing helmets back in those days. And if they did, it was just something to tie your goggles to. It didn't prevent any cracked skulls. Some of the spectators would pour water on him, and he'd take off again. The fifth time he did it, they didn't bother waking him up."

Coveralls for uniforms. Service station shirts for certification of employment. Cornfield race tracks and worse. A $25 purse, with $10 going to the winner, was big enough reason to whip somebody, one way or another. "I saw a driver whup the daylights out of his mechanic one time in 1950 'cause his mechanic forgot the lug wrench," says one old-timer. "He didn't have a flat tire. The driver was mad 'cause he didn't have anything to fight with after the race."

Crazy or hungry, they stretched heavy chains over the limbs of moss-draped oaks to form a lift for engines. Shade-tree mechanics they came to be called. Rough and ready but fast developing skills for pulling a little more horsepower out of an engine. Discovering something new through experiments with springs, with thicknesses, with tolerances, with clearances.

Then along came NASCAR to pump a little respectability into a sport that needed it worse than a country boy needed a bath come

Saturday. Big, bright William H. G. (Bill) France had raced a little himself. Raced some for prize money he never saw. France steered NASCAR through a trying infancy, but it was NASCAR's continuing role that led to the great stock car racing names known today.

Bill France was born in Horseshoe, Virginia, but the first time he hauled any horsepower was in high school. Big Bill tossed his six-foot four-inch frame around the basketball court for Washington, D.C.'s Central High School.

France packed his earthly belongings and headed for Florida, where he became a filling station operator in Daytona Beach. It was France and others interested in stock car racing who formed NASCAR and stuck with it through thick and thin to make its drivers the best-known stock car jockeys of all time.

The formative years did not pass without problems. There were heated driver disqualifications. Rules were made to be broken and more than once NASCAR was charged with unfair tactics, for reasons stretching from rules interpretations to on-the-track partiality.

In 1959 Bob Talbert, writing for *The State* newspaper in Columbia, South Carolina, stated, "Stock car racing has succeeded in spite of itself. In spite of petty bickering. In spite of petty prejudices. In spite of inconsistent rules. The sport has succeeded because the people of the South have no other major-league sport with which to identify."

The construction of Darlington International Raceway in 1949 and the ensuing marriage to NASCAR gave birth to the concept of superspeedways which was to flourish some ten years later. Yet the roots were planted by men who drove the stockers at tracks like the old fairgrounds at Charlotte, North Carolina, or the Lakewood Speedway in Atlanta, Georgia, or the fairgrounds at Greensboro, North Carolina. By those drivers who roared their way through the red clay of a track in Martinsville, Virginia, or those who maneuvered the tricky corners of such long-gone tracks as Princess Anne Speedway in Norfolk, Virginia.

None of those drivers paved any roads for sissies. They did it the hard way. The tough way. They did it in daredevil style. And often, in humorous style. Because of their flair for fun they left more than one irate local citizen or businessman in their tireprints.

Joe Weatherly, dubbed the "Clown Prince of Stock Car Racing" by Talbert, left a trail of legends local libraries would have a hard time containing. It was Weatherly and another colorful driver of the late Fifties and early Sixties, L. D. Austin, who left behind the legend of U-Wreck-Its in southern stock car circles.

Weatherly, so the story goes, had a penchant for parking rental cars in unusual places prior to leaving a city following an event. Typical of Weatherly's style was the conversation that reportedly took place in an airport lobby following a race one night. Weatherly, speaking to the counterman for the rental-car agency, said, "I want to turn in the keys to my rental car."

"Okay, Mr. Weatherly," said the polite representative. "Did you leave the car out front?"

"Oh no," said little Joe. "I rode out with some friends. Left the car at the motel, Pops."

"Okay," said the polite representative, "just sign right here."

Weatherly signed and turned to leave. "By the way, Pops, when your guy goes to pick up the car, better tell him to take along some scuba-diving gear. I missed the parking lot last night."

The car was found with the front end submerged in the shallow end of the swimming pool.

Austin, kidding the people at NASCAR registration, reportedly listed Avis as his car owner when he signed in for a race. "I'm driving a U-Crash-It," he told them when asked what type of car he was driving.

The legends come entwined with the truth. Take a tale of truth and stretch it a bit—then you have a legend. One driver showed up at a race one time in a brand-new car, ready to make a qualifying attempt. After one lap on the track, a spectator came running down to the starter's stand screaming, "That's my car he's in out there." Turned out the guy was president of a local finance company and had signed the papers on the car that same morning. The race driver quickly answered, "Well, you don't think I'd drive my own car in one of these things, do you? Why, you could tear a car up in a race like this."

Stock car racing has also had its share of hair-raising moments in the old wooden grandstands. They showed a definite tendency to burn, as an estimated two thousand race fans who were comfortably seated in the Greensboro, North Carolina, fairgrounds bleachers on May 1, 1955, would attest. History records it as the hottest day in the life of the fairgrounds track. The bleachers burned down. The fire, whipped through the aging structure by strong winds, destroyed sixteen cars, three trucks and one motorcycle. Veteran Greensboro announcer Bob Montgomery was credited with saving the lives of spectators who filed from the fiery structure in good order. Four fans received minor burns. A similar grandstand fire claimed the bleachers at a Wilson, North Carolina, track also, where announcer Ray Melton of Virginia Beach, Virginia, maintained order over the public address system.

Tales of the early days range from those of violence to those of leg-slapping hillbilly humor. One driver who was banged into the guard rail by another became so incensed he got his race car moving again, drove it back to the pits and told his crew chief to hand him his pistol. He went back on the track, pulled up alongside the offending driver and fired a couple of shots. The bullets went through the thin metal shell just behind the driver's seat. The car smashed straight into a wall. The gun-toting driver returned to the pits, parked his race car, hid his pistol and swore he knew nothing of the bullet holes in the other driver's car.

He later told friends, "You've got to let these drivers know you're serious. If you don't, they'll run all over you." To which his friend replied, "I reckon the only way you could have let him know you were any more serious would have been to shoot him instead of the car."

Drivers on the dust bowls of the early days went so far as to dump sugar in competitors' gas tanks. Lugs were loosened, causing a wheel to come flying off. Let just enough air out of a tire and the driver would spin the first time he tried to steer the ill-handling machine through a corner.

They did it all. It was certainly no sport for the faint of heart. Nor was it a sport for those without a sense of humor. Like the time at Atlanta's old Lakewood Speedway. "We had to have all our drivers cleared by the police department," says an old-line promoter. "About all it took to declare yourself a race driver back in those days was a car, a driving helmet, a black jacket, a pair of boots and a drink of hard liquor, preferably of local stock."

Lakewood, at the time, was owned by the city. To prevent undesirables such as suspected bootleg liquor haulers from racing, the city police required a list of the names of entries prior to each race.

"Lots of times," says the old promoter, "drivers would sign in under some other name. They'd be wanted by police for questioning about hauling moonshine liquor or something of the sort. They'd sign some fictitious name. One night, the police came over and wanted us to stop the race. They said the leader was wanted for questioning, and they had a warrant for his arrest. We stopped the race so they could go get him and that was the funniest thing I ever saw. He sensed something was wrong when we stopped the race and there wasn't a crash or anything. He never slowed down.

"The police were running up and down the track, waving their pistols and hollering for him to stop, and the crowd was cheering him on. He was zigging in and out of those policemen. Never did hit one of them, and they couldn't afford to shoot because they might hit somebody in the crowd. That old boy's mechanics ran across the track and opened the gate on the backstretch leading out to the street. Last time anybody saw him, he was heading down a city street into the dark. The crowd loved it."

Detroit's manufacturers, the men behind the machines driven by the men people pay to see, played leapfrog with the sport and NASCAR throughout the years. In and out. Believing in it. Not believing in it. Supporting it. Not supporting it.

Actually, the factory teams appeared for the first time at Daytona Beach, Florida, for Speed Weeks in 1956. Sandy Grady wrote, "Here, in 1956, the Detroit auto manufacturers fought their first battle in the war of stock car racing."

Daytona became a "hot, jealous battlefield for the big car makers of America. Each hoped to leave with a booty of advertising prestige." There were more vice-presidents running around on the sandy beach than race drivers. Pat Purcell, France's right-hand man and one of the guiding forces behind NASCAR's success, told his boss, "Bill, the only way you'll possibly keep them all happy is to give them all a trophy." France, however, chose to let them have at it, a practice he has maintained for the most part.

The same old argument, factory sponsorships versus independent sponsorships, has been bounced around over the years more than many of the stiff-springed machines. After Speed Weeks in 1956, Bob Brown, obviously a stock car fan, wrote a letter to the editors of *Speed Age* magazine, stating, "Two years ago, if someone asked Ford or Pontiac to sponsor a car, they would have laughed in his face, but now they are using the sport to promote sales. As soon as the fad of horsepower and performance is over, they will drop it like a hot potato." Brown also asked, "What chance will the private entries have against factory-sponsored teams? Private owners did, after all, start the whole thing. Ford and the others never did anything to help the sport when asked, why should NASCAR do anything for them now?"

The ever-present voice of factory opposition then added, "The big companies will milk the good sport at will, and push it aside when they feel like it. Meanwhile, false and misleading claims will be flying high and low."

To this day, proponents of factory sponsorship quickly claim such participation and added exposure serves to enhance the sport in the eye of the public. The car-buying public, at that.

Throughout it all, men have emerged as heroes behind the wheel of stock racing cars, the kind you drive to work, if in name only. Maybe the Dodge on the track today doesn't look like the one you crawl down the expressway in each morning, but it's a Dodge nonetheless.

And the men behind the wheel command respect. It is no easy task to hang onto a steering wheel at 200 miles an hour just an inch or two away from a car staring back at you through the front windshield and another just as close out the back. It is no easy task to turn the wheel by whiskers when the slightest mistake might cost a life, your own or that of someone racing against you.

This is the story of the cars that carry the names. Buick, Dodge, Plymouth, Ford, Mercury, Chrysler, T-Bird, Henry-J, Cadillac, Lincoln, Oldsmobile, Pontiac, Chevrolet, Hudson, Studebaker, Nash. All the cars that plowed and sped their way from the back-woods roads to the rumbling dirt tracks and onto the nation's superspeedways of today. The Grand National Cars—highly modified late-model American sedans.

More importantly, this is the story of the men who drove them. This is the story of the men who "made" the machines. Guys who devoted a lifetime to turning left and standing on it. As Lee Petty once told son Richard, who has now earned more than a million dollars strapped behind the wheel of the same kind of car you now drive to work or once did, "Take the good with the bad."

There's plenty of both but one thing's for sure. Stock car racing is no sport for sissies.

1 THE FORD DRIVERS

Henry Ford wrote his brother in the early 1900s, "I can make dollars racing when I can't make cents manufacturing." Ole Henry was no fool when it came to catching people's attention. He took a Ford across the ice on Lake St. Clair near Detroit for a world's record in 1904. He was in Daytona Beach, Florida, a year later for speed runs. Ford, in some shape or fashion, has been at it ever since. And men driving Fords have become some of stock car racing's best-known stars.

Obviously, somebody high in Ford's executive offices didn't like the record of NASCAR's first seven years of Grand National stock car events. Those were lean years for the pioneer manufacturer credited with designing a V8 engine to fit a standard car for

They called him Gentleman Ned Jarrett but he was anything but a gentleman on the Grand National tracks. Jarrett won the championship for Ford for the first time in NASCAR history.

the average pocketbook. Then in 1956 Ford officials hit the beach in Daytona like an invasion force. Ford banners and pennants flew like bullets. Ford division representatives alone numbered over thirty that year at Speed Weeks.

Ford failed to win that first outing at Daytona. However, Ford stock cars have won more Grand National events than any other make since that year. Some of the best stock car drivers in the world have ridden them to the checkered flag more than 280 times in twenty-two years of Grand National competition. Red Byron, the former midget car driver who won NASCAR's first point championship, flat-footed a Ford in many races, although his championship was claimed in an Oldsmobile. Little Joe Weatherly, Curtis Turner, Glenn (Fireball) Roberts, Junior Johnson. Name a driver with a stock car name, and chances are he sat down at one time or another in a Ford.

The man known best for brilliant performances in a Ford is Fred Lorenzen, a hard-driving, hardworking ex-carpenter from Chicago's suburb of Elmhurst, Illinois. Lorenzen came South the hard way. He won the United States Auto Club's stock car championship a couple of times before trying his hand with the big-money NASCAR boys. "I remember the first time he came to

Atlanta," says Alf Knight, general superintendent of Atlanta International Raceway since its beginning in 1959. "All he had was a beat-up old Ford race car. No money. No place to sleep. He stayed here a week before one of our races, working on his old car, getting it ready. I think he finished in twenty-sixth spot. He told me when he left that time he'd never be back unless he had a car capable of winning. And when he came back, he did."

Lorenzen was sitting at home during the winter, fearing he might have to go back to driving nails instead of stock cars when the phone rang prior to the 1961 season. An angel was calling. Courtesy of Ford. Ralph Moody, half the famed Charlotte, North Carolina, firm that was gaining a reputation for building fast Fords, asked Lorenzen to drive the Holman-Moody machine. Thus one of the sport's most successful teams was formed. Lorenzen quickly captured the respect of competitors and spectators alike.

LEFT: *Well-known A. J. Foyt, who frequently drives a Ford in Grand National races, is popular with stock car fans even though best known for his three Indianapolis "500" victories.* RIGHT: *Donnie Allison, a three-time modified champion, won several Grand National events in the late Sixties driving a Ford.*

It was in Darlington, South Carolina, at the Rebel 300 in May of 1961 that Lorenzen made his mark. He made it on one of the most respected competitors of all time. Battling for the lead on the archaic track that treats drivers like unwanted suitors, Lorenzen tried to get past the leader, none other than Curtis Turner himself. Moody, standing in the hot pits, knew what to expect. He had driven against Turner himself. Moody had banged bumpers with Turner at Daytona's old beach-and-road course. Moody, in fact, had been top Ford qualifier at Daytona in 1956 when the factory wave from Detroit landed. He won a total of five races for Ford before taking off the seat belt and trading it for a coaching position in the pits.

As Lorenzen, Ralph Moody's protégé, diced with Turner for position, Moody probably whispered to himself, "Now's the time. If he's gonna be a race driver, now's the time to prove it." Lorenzen tried to pass Turner on the inside. Turner cut him off. The Illinois native waited a lap and tried to get by on Turner's outside. Turner almost squeezed him into the wall. Lorenzen, realizing time was running out with just a few laps remaining, set the old pro up. He faked him to the outside like a good broken-field runner, then streaked past on the inside and held Turner off to win his first major stock car race. It was far from being his last.

It was a lot different from the previous times Lorenzen had competed in the South. He had ventured below the Mason-Dixon line once before the 1959 season when he returned home broke, downhearted and wondering what to do. That time, in 1956, he made seven races and went home with his pockets turned inside out. His total earnings for the 1956 NASCAR season were $235.

Lorenzen won the Atlanta 500 in 1962 and finished well in the money at every event the Holman-Moody team chose to enter. In 1963 and 1964 Lorenzen lost his carpenter's trademark. Fans referred to the young bachelor as "Ford's Golden Boy" and "Fearless Freddie." He won the Atlanta 500 both years. In 1963 he became the first stock car driver in history to earn more than $100,000 in a season.

Lorenzen staged many stirring duels with Plymouth-driving

Fearless Fred Lorenzen, Ford's "Golden Boy," was the darling of fans during stock car racing's roaring duels of the Sixties. Lorenzen won every event but the Southern 500, a race he grew up listening to on the radio in his Illinois home.

A. J. Foyt (right) *explains a fine point of stock car racing to veteran Indy driver Jim Hurtubise, who won the Atlanta 500 in a Plymouth in 1964.*

*Rebel driver Bobby Lee was one of the Ford drivers in the 160-mile
Grand National race on the Daytona beach-and-road course in 1958.
Stock car fans thrilled to the sliding cars as they buzzed through the
sandy turns broadside.*

superstar Richard Petty. A three-time winner of the Atlanta 500,
winner of Charlotte's World 600 and National 500, winner of
Daytona's prestigious 500-miler, Lorenzen had left few stock car
victory lanes untouched by the wheels of his famed silver and blue
No. 28 when he retired in 1967 after running only a few races that
year.

He had won twenty-six Grand National events at the time of his
retirement and most had been on the high-speed, high-banked
superspeedways. He had earned more than $400,000 in less than
ten years. Yet one race eluded Ford's Golden Boy. The Southern
500. The granddaddy of them all. The oldest stock car race on the
circuit. Torn by ulcers from the pressures of having to win week
in and week out, Fearless Freddie quit. The blond bachelor from
Elmhurst had had enough. He wanted to quit while on top. His
good friend and the driver he most admired, Glenn (Fireball)

Roberts, had died as a result of burns received in a fiery Charlotte crash in 1964. Other friends had died. Billy Wade. Jimmy Pardue. Little Joe Weatherly. Lorenzen took a vacation. Skied in Aspen, Colorado. Fished for blue marlin in the Gulf. Did some commentary for ABC's "Wide World of Sports." All the time, promoters nagged him to return to the scenes of his greatest triumphs. Lorenzen didn't listen, but retirement bored him. He had invested his money wisely in stocks. There was no need to return. However, Charlotte's Richard Howard talked him into returning in 1970. Freddie ran well but failed to win. He drove for several different people, in several different makes. Finally, in September of 1971 Lorenzen returned to Darlington in a Wood brothers Ford product that was capable of winning. Fearless Freddie knew it was a chance to win the Southern 500, the only big race that had escaped him.

Fred Lorenzen, now thirty-four, was thinking to boyhood days. Labor Day. The Southern 500. "It's the one race I've always wanted to win," he often said. "It was the only stock car race you ever heard of up in Elmhurst. I always listened to it on the radio. I always wanted to drive in it and I always wanted to win it." Now, after several years' retirement, Lorenzen had another chance to win the big one, the Masters of stock car racing. He knew the

Favorite Alfred (Speedy) Thompson (46) prepares to pass a Ford driven by Phil Orr on the north turn of Daytona's old 4.1-mile beach-and-road course.

Wood brothers-prepared car could put him in victory lane. "When I was down in Florida for that first year, away from the tracks completely, I couldn't stand it on Labor Day," he said a few months before Darlington's famed race. "I had to turn on the radio while we were out in the boat. I couldn't stand it. I knew that day I had to try it at least one more time."

Lorenzen drove the fast machine around the slick, treacherous Darlington oval with the reckless abandon he had used to blow past Curtis Turner. He drove farther and farther into the corners during practice. He pressed the accelerator down quicker coming off the corners. His confidence rose. So did his speed. Fearless Freddie, the crowd favorite, was back. He would be a contender for the coveted pole position. He could set fast time. Shades of the old days. Shades of the days when the fidgety, nervous bachelor was the driver feared most by NASCAR's best. But Freddie didn't make it into the starting field. He pushed the car a little too hard coming off the superslippery fourth turn. It spun and crashed into the inside retaining wall, cutting a flagpole in half. Lorenzen was rushed to a hospital in Florence, South Carolina, some ten miles away, his dreams of a Southern 500 trophy ended once again. Lorenzen, however, is still the Golden Boy to Ford fans throughout the world. Fearless Freddie, they call him. And rightly so.

Ford threw a retirement party for him in 1967 and Holman-Moody announced it would never again run the No. 28 or the silver

Glenn (Fireball) Roberts, a hometown favorite, leads Curtis Turner

and blue color scheme on a car. While Lorenzen might have been the most publicized driver in Ford's racing history, other drivers are well known for their stock car exploits in Ford machines. Gentleman Ned Jarrett, one of the most popular drivers in NASCAR history, gave Ford its first NASCAR championship.

Jarrett, who grew up in Conover, North Carolina, son of a lumberman, became addicted to cars at an early age. But his dad didn't want him racing. Jarrett's father wanted his son to spend his days as a bookkeeper watching pages go by rather than guard rails at 200 miles an hour. Ned, however, had notions not uncommon to little boys with big ideas. And he worked to achieve his goals. Jarrett raced in dust-bowl events under an assumed name so his father wouldn't find out. When Poppa Jarrett did discover his son was racing, he told him, "If you're going to race, be the best at it."

Ned Jarrett was. His first Grand National car was purchased with the utmost in confidence. Jarrett went to a local banker and borrowed the money for his car. He told his banker he would pay the money back after the weekend. A short-term loan was all he wanted. He got it. There were three short-track Grand National events over the weekend. Ned figured if he won them all, he could pay the money back. He did. "I got to thinking in the last one about what I would do if the car blew an engine or something of that sort, or crashed," says Ned, "and it worried me half to

down the beach straightaway during the 1956 Daytona Beach race.

Ford driver Fred Lorenzen (left) *and Mercury driver Darel Dieringer* (right) *chat with golfing great Sam Snead during the annual Pure-Darlington Record Club banquet prior to the famed Labor Day Southern 500. Snead was guest speaker at the banquet.*

death the last few laps. But you can't think that way and drive a stock car. You've got to believe you can win." Jarrett did believe. In some fifteen years of Grand National driving he became the sport's fourth-biggest winner with fifty victories, a distinction he holds today with the fabled leadfoot, Junior Johnson.

Jarrett captured the Grand National championship for Ford in 1965, driving for DuPont heir Bondy Long of Camden, South Carolina. It wasn't the first time Ned won the championship; he had driven a Chevrolet to the title in 1961. His biggest victories were the Dixie 500 in 1964 and the 1965 Southern 500. Jarrett's victories were not limited to the race track. He spoke to civic groups, spent time with thousands of fans, voiced his views of the sport to high school students and spread the dignified word about stock car racing everywhere he traveled—and he never charged a nickel. "There's more to a sport than just driving a race car," he often said. "A man should always want to better his profession in any way he can." Ned did just what his father had told him. He mastered his field before he retired, after the 1965 season.

Jarrett is still involved with the sport to which he contributed so much during his days as an active, winning driver. He is general manager of the Hickory Speedway in North Carolina and also serves as color announcer on the Universal Racing Network, along with veteran motor-sports journalist Hank Schoolfield and one of the nation's leading racing announcers, Hal Hamrick.

Former tank driver Nelson Stacy burned his name into the memory of Ford fans with a bright yellow machine that left blisters of embarrassment on some of NASCAR's best competitors during the 1961 and 1962 seasons. Stacy, who ran the Midwestern stock car circuit for many years before landing a ride in a Holman-Moody machine, became an overnight hero with his Southern 500 victory. It was quite unusual, to say the least. Apparently Stacy figured he could whip a race car around the old oval in much the same manner he had wrestled a Sherman tank. He did the impossible, passing Marvin Panch in the most feared corner in stock car racing, Darlington's third turn. At the time the third turn at Darlington was virtually flat and passing was impossible because the groove allowed room for only one car. If a machine tried to pass another entering the tight turn, it was forced into the guard rail with terrific impact because of the turn's narrow, flat contour. Stacy, gunning for his first big win, manhandled his canary yellow machine down

Little Joe Weatherly, the "Clown Prince of Stock Car Racing," was always smiling. He was one of the first drivers to win a Grand National event in a Ford. He later won races in many other makes.

below Panch's car just a few laps from the finish of the long grind, bounced off the rail, turned sideways, regained control and raced home the winner. His courageous (some drivers chose to call it otherwise) victory is still considered one of the most exciting in Darlington's long history. It is also one of the most popular since Stacy became known as a down-to-earth guy as well as a fearless driver. Stacy, a grandfather by the time he won the Southern 500, won the Rebel 300 and Charlotte's World 600 the following year. He started the 1963 season, but a couple of serious accidents forced the hard-charging, soft-spoken Stacy to retire.

Marvin Panch, a quiet Floridian who let his driving do his talking, was another Ford driver who found the way to victory lane. Called by many stock veterans the most consistent driver to put on a helmet, Panch won seventeen Grand National events in a career that spanned more than twenty years. Pancho, as he was known, amazed veterans with his ability to turn laps within hundredths of a second, lap after lap after lap. "He drives a race car right to the ragged edge," Duzzie Larick once said at Darlington, "and then he mashes a button in his head that keeps it right there."

Panch won at three superspeedways—Charlotte, Daytona and twice at Atlanta. He was also acknowledged as one of stock car racing's smoothest performers on a road course. A sports car, however, contributed greatly to Panch's retirement. He was blazing around Daytona International Speedway in a Maserati during Speed Weeks preparations in 1963 when the Maserati crashed, bursting into flame. Big Tiny Lund and four others pulled Panch from the flaming wreckage and were later credited with saving his life.

Panch had been scheduled to drive a Wood brothers car in the 500, but he recommended that Lund be given a chance; Lund took advantage of the break and won the 1963 race. Panch recovered after many months and returned to the cockpit. He won the 1965 Dixie 500 with relief help from A. J. Foyt but then retired when recurring problems with the burns he suffered two years before made it impossible for him to continue. Panch is still a well-known figure at the nation's race tracks. He serves as a consultant to the

LEFT: *Joe Weatherly's face was scarred but the little guy from Norfolk, Virginia, was always quick to point out he received the injury on the highway rather than the race track. He died following a crash at Riverside, California, in 1964.* RIGHT: *Legendary Curtis (Pops) Turner was on the factory Ford team and was known for his heavy foot and daredevil style. He won Grand National races in practically every kind of car, including a Nash Rambler.*

Grey-Rock Corporation and works with Grand National competitors in setting up and adjusting the valuable brakes they must have to slow down a 4,000-pound machine running speeds up to 200 mph.

Curtis Turner never ran less than 200 miles an hour, on or off the race track. Once barred from NASCAR competition, this native of Roanoke, Virginia, became the focal point of more legends than any stock car driver. Turner is credited with seventeen Grand National victories. Before he was banned from competition for his part in attempting to unionize drivers, he drove to one superspeedway win, whipping a 1956 Ford to victory lane in the Southern 500. Turner's fan appeal, however, came from the dirt tracks. The tall, wavy-haired Virginian slung a stock car through the dirt track corners with reckless abandon. His style of pushing a race car made him everyone's all-American. "Nobody could fling a car around a track like Turner," says Jim Foster, a former Spartanburg, South Carolina, sports editor and now NASCAR public relations director. "Turner would cross his car up about the start-finish line and stomp on the gas. The car would sling dirt twenty feet high in the air, like a powerboat leaving a rooster tail. Turner drove like he was on the verge of losing control in every corner and the fans loved it."

Turner was ousted from NASCAR in 1961. He continued, as he had for many years, to deal in the profession known as his second love. Turner's speculative timber deals are known far and wide. They called him the "millionaire lumberman." Legends grew from deals in which he made a million dollars one day and sold out the next. Turner became the first stock car driver to bridge a generation gap when, in 1965, after being away from the sport for more than four years, he returned to drive in a 500-mile race at North Carolina Motor Speedway. New race fans had only the legend, but Turner proved fact is as much a part of legend as fiction. He drove to victory in a Ford. The young fans then realized why Turner had always been characterized as the "Babe Ruth of Stock Car Racing." He further backed up his title by becoming the first stock car driver to top 180 miles an hour at Daytona International Speedway in winning the pole position for the 1967 Daytona 500 at an average speed of 180.831 miles an hour.

Turner, who called everyone "Pops," was actually a member of Ford's first factory team when he and his good Virginia buddy Joe Weatherly agreed to drive 1957 Fords with manufacturer support. The parties at his home in Charlotte, North Carolina, became famous in his last years when he opened the doors to anyone wanting to attend—he loved people and loved racing. Following his win at North Carolina Motor Speedway in 1965, Turner was asked what he would do next. "Well, I see no reason why we shouldn't

Dick Hutcherson of Keokuk, Iowa, burst on the Grand National scene in the late Sixties and won several events.

Former tire changer Darel Dieringer hitched a ride in Junior Johnson's Ford for a portion of a Grand National season but Dieringer achieved his lifelong goal of winning the Southern 500 in a Mercury.

start a brand-new party and everybody's invited," he replied.

Turner's attitude and free-swinging style kept him in constant hot water with various government agencies. The FAA found no humor in the report that Turner landed his airplane at a small town shopping center to let off a friend. He also landed his plane on many speedway straightaways, much to the dismay of local officials. One prominent member of a business community remem-

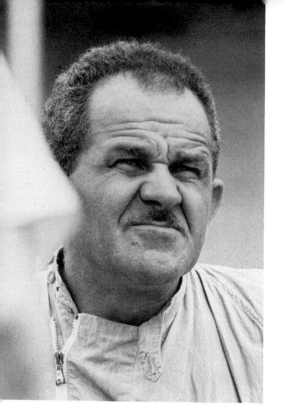

LEFT: *Wendell Scott of Danville, Virginia, is the only Negro driver ever to win a Grand National event. Scott, a veteran driver, has been on the NASCAR scene for more than twenty years in a Ford.*

BELOW: *Cale Yarborough's first big break came when he landed a ride in Herman (The Turtle) Beam's Ford, but he made his winning name in a Ford and Mercury with No. 21, owned by the Wood brothers of Stuart, Virginia.*

BOTTOM: *Glenn (Fireball) Roberts' last big victory was in a Ford he drove home well ahead of the field in the 1963 Southern 500 at Darlington. Pontiac fans cringed when Roberts switched to Ford.*

bers a time when Turner told him he wanted to show him a tract of timber. The two jumped into Turner's plane and took off. Turner showed him the property and en route home to Charlotte spotted a short track with time trials under way. They landed and went to the track. "Curtis told me he'd be back in a few minutes," the businessman recalls. "Next thing I knew they were announcing him as the driver of the lead car in the feature race. He won the race and gave all the money to the car owner, and thanked him for letting him drive his car." Turner reportedly won more than 350 stock car races before he died in an airplane crash in 1970.

Little Joe Weatherly was Curtis Turner's friend, constant companion and fiercest competitor when the two Virginians hooked up with the Ford factory team. Weatherly, a two-time national motorcycle champion, drove the dirt tracks like his buddy and developed an equal flair for off-track fun. Weatherly's fun-loving earned him the title "Clown Prince of Stock Car Racing." He drove many makes of cars with equal success, but Weatherly's popularity with fans developed during his Ford-driving days prior to 1961. Little Joe won the 1960 Rebel 300 in a Ford, and many of his twenty-four Grand National victories resulted from the partnership between him and the factory-financed Ford.

Weatherly, a short, kinky-haired daredevil who used to ride a motorcycle through the streets of Norfolk standing on the seat, wore black and white saddle oxfords, golf gloves and a bright-colored Darlington shirt. This outfit was his trademark for years. In addition to his skill behind the wheel, Weatherly was a master at coining phrases. He originated the term "flat out and belly to the ground," which was his way of saying the only way to drive a stock car was just as fast as it would go. He called Indianapolis-type cars "cucumbers on hayraker wheels." He hated the color green, figuring it was bad luck except at the payoff window. Weatherly once made a motel owner give him a different room when he discovered the walls in his room were painted green. The No. 13 and peanuts in the pits were also unlucky. He drove No. 8 and explained with characteristic Weatherly humor, "That way, the fans can always tell where I am, even if I'm upside down."

Former Californian Marvin Panch was considered one of the most consistent drivers in Grand National competition. He drove many different makes of car during a long career in which he won seventeen major events.

Ralph Moody, who later became Fred Lorenzen's instructor for Grand National competition, was one of Ford's first factory-supported drivers. In this particular race, Moody did not fare so well.

Fords were well represented in NASCAR's old convertible division, which ran the Rebel 300 at Darlington as its big event each year. Ned Jarrett (11) leads Nelson Stacy (29) and Marvin Panch (21) through Darlington's tricky first turn during the Rebel race.

He was the master of the practical joke. He carried a rubber snake with him always, and he originated the "mongoose" trick, which he enjoyed immensely. The mongoose was a piece of animal fur tied to a spring within a cage. Weatherly would go to great lengths explaining the fierceness of his little "animal." Then, once his practical joke victim was thoroughly convinced of the mongoose's fury, Weatherly would lead him to the cage. When the unsuspecting party leaned over to take a closer look at the vicious little animal, Weatherly would trip the spring and the piece of fur would fly out in the face of his victim, scaring him out of his wits, and Weatherly would howl. The joke backfired on Weatherly one day in the office of Darlington Raceway's president Bob Colvin. Colvin, a close friend of Weatherly's throughout his racing years, clued Weatherly's victim in on the joke, and when little Joe sprang the trap, the victim whipped out a pistol loaded with blanks and began firing. His joke having backfired, Weatherly never played it again.

Weatherly's wit was unmatchable. He liked to aim the needle at other drivers, particularly those outside stock car racing, and fire off a Weatherly expression, such as "them foreign sporty car drivers with the big vocabularies." He did it with no malice intended. He talked, as Bob Talbert once wrote, "in shorthand." Although Weatherly won only two so-called major races, he twice won the NASCAR championship, in 1962 and 1963. He won his first title in a Pontiac, the second in Mercurys, cars he referred to as "overgrown Fords with buggy springs." Since his car owner at the time, Bud Moore of Spartanburg, South Carolina, did not choose to run anything but the longer, bigger-paying races, Weatherly earned the championship by showing up at many of the shorter races to borrow a ride. He drove the wheels off anything he could put his golf gloves on to earn his second title. Weatherly died in a 1963 crash at Riverside International Raceway in California. His last ride through the streets of his native Norfolk for once had people crying.

The man who must go down as the all-time hard-luck driver in NASCAR history spent most of his driving days in a Ford. Larry Frank was an ex-Marine from Greenville, South Carolina. If he had a fault, it was one race fans have always appreciated. Larry Frank knew only one way to race. Out front. Flat out. If the fastest way around a track was bouncing off the guard rail in every turn, Frank took it. He drove to the front of virtually every race he ever entered. Yet Frank could not find the machine to withstand the pace he chose to set. In 1962, as Labor Day and the Southern

Nelson Stacy, a former tank driver, took a liking to Darlington as a rookie and won the Southern 500 in 1961. His canary yellow Ford No. 29 was a fan favorite for several seasons.

Racing is not always fun, as Dick Johnson finds out. Notice the front wheels turned in the opposite direction of the slide. Johnson was not injured in this slide at Charlotte Motor Speedway.

500 at Darlington approached, Larry Frank had no Grand National victories to show for more than fifteen years behind the wheel. Frank drove his Ford with blind fury that hot, humid Labor Day and knew he had it won, but the checkered flag fell on Junior Johnson's car. Frank, totally dejected, parked his Ford off the fourth-turn apron of the track. He climbed out, refusing to believe he had not won. He wiped the sweat and grime from his face and walked over to the infield fence where he talked with fans. Late that night a recheck of NASCAR's scoring proved Frank *had* won the race—only to be deprived of the moment of crowning glory all drivers wait to enjoy. It was the only Grand National victory Frank was to achieve, but he will long be remembered as the driver who won but was forced to find victory lane a day late.

While Ford drivers were making names for themselves by going faster than anything else in town, at least one of them made a name for himself by driving slowly. Slower than anyone else in town. Herman Beam never won a race, though he always hoped he would. Race fans of the late Fifties and early Sixties recall him as

Little Joe Weatherly, wearing his familiar Darlington shirt, takes off his trademark saddle oxfords to cool his feet after falling out of a race. Weatherly, always superstitious, took his socks off a few minutes later when they turned green under the water. The only green he liked was that they handed out at the payoffs.

Marvin (Pancho) Panch was quiet but his driving in the Wood brothers No. 21 did some loud talking for Ford.

Herman (The Turtle) Beam. Herman was a University of North Carolina graduate with a degree in chemistry. His formula for stock car racing was outlasting the front-runners, making more laps than they did by race's end. He would establish a pace in one of the slower grooves on the track and drive all day. Race fans loved the little guy from Johnson City, Tennessee. They were constantly betting among themselves that Herman The Turtle would finish higher in the final rundown than such chargers as Fireball

LEFT: *Larry Frank won only one race. However, Frank did not receive the normal victory lane salute. All he received was a handshake and a word of encouragement from an infield spectator. Junior Johnson was given the checkered flag for the 1962 Southern 500 but a scoring recheck proved Frank the winner the following day.*

In 1969 Richard Petty, who had previously raced nothing but Plymouths, switched to Ford because Plymouth was pulling out of racing. Petty won ten races that year and finished third in the championship standings, but returned to Plymouth the following year.

Roberts, Joe Weatherly and others who set the fast pace for long events. More than once Herman finished races well ahead of the chargers. Perhaps his finest hour in stock car racing, though, did not result from Herman's driving but his role as a car owner. Tired of being called The Turtle, Herman turned the driving over to a youngster named Cale Yarborough from Timmonsville, South Carolina, for a 100-mile dirt track race at Concord, North Carolina, in 1963. Yarborough, later to become one of Mercury's biggest stars, put Herman's car out front. For the first time a race was run with The Turtle's car leading the way. Herman Beam flashed the biggest smile of his career as Yarborough showed the field the way. The car eventually ran hot and dropped back, but Herman Beam was smiling—they wouldn't call him The Turtle anymore.

Banjo Matthews was a far cry from Herman Beam. The only thing the two Ford drivers had in common was a lack of Grand National victories. Matthews showed his rear bumper to as many drivers as anyone, but the Asheville, North Carolina, driver never found victory lane in Grand National competition. Matthews was a

46

Ford-fan favorite for his run-up-front-or-don't-run-at-all philosophy. Matthews' twenty-year driving career is typified by his luck at Atlanta International Raceway in the 1961 Dixie 400. Matthews' Ford held the lead for 143 laps and appeared destined for victory lane when the engine blew just five laps from the finish line. Such luck rode in the cockpit with Matthews throughout his Grand National career. He retired with his name prominently etched in the record book for the qualifying records he established with regularity. History might not record Matthews as a winner, but it will certainly recall him in terms race fans constantly discuss. If Matthews' machines had matched his durability, he certainly would have won more than his share of Grand National events.

David Pearson won three NASCAR Grand National championships in four years, a feat unequaled in twenty-three years of NASCAR competition. Pearson's first championship came in 1966 at the wheel of a Dodge. He then switched to a Ford and won again in 1968 and 1969. In 1970 he drove a '69 Ford Torino (above) *and a '70 Torino Cobra* (below) *in only nineteen races instead of the fifty-one he had entered the year before. He finished twenty-third in the point standings but won over $87,000 by finishing in the top five places in nine races.*

Another Ford driver who quickly earned a name for himself on the Grand National scene is Dick Hutcherson, a native of Keokuk, Iowa, who burst onto the southern scene with an unbelievable debut. Hutcherson entered a 100-mile dirt race at South Carolina's Columbia Speedway for his first outing before southern fans. He took the lead in the race as soon as the green flag waved and couldn't be beaten. Hutcherson was a master of dirt driving, having toured the Midwestern stock car circuit for several years. He won fourteen events in a brief NASCAR career that included a 1967 Dixie 500 victory at Atlanta International Raceway. He retired from driving to become a team manager for Holman-Moody.

2 THE PLYMOUTH DRIVERS

Plymouth and Petty and popularity—the three go together, they always have. Furys, fortune and fame belong to the Petty family. Plymouth stock car racing fans will tell you so without batting an eyelash. Travel the heartland of stock car racing and you'll see more blue Plymouth passenger cars than any other make. Petty blue. Plymouth buyers swear by the Pettys—for good reason. There has been, since 1949, no stock car racing team as successful as that of the Pettys. The North Carolina Pettys—the stock car rockets from Randleman.

The Petty family debut in Grand National competition was made in spectacular, if not winning, fashion. And it was made in the family car, a Plymouth that Poppa Lee Petty proceeded to roll

Lee Petty, of Randleman, North Carolina, had no peers in a stock car. The three-time Grand National champion of NASCAR turned the family car over in his first race but everything was uphill for the Petty name from that time on.

four times in the first Grand National event ever held, a dirt race at the old Charlotte, North Carolina, fairgrounds. Poppa Lee might have rolled the family car four times in his first race, but the Petty name has been rolling up victories ever since. And, for the most part, the father of Richard Petty made his name in a Plymouth. As early as 1951 and 1952, Lee Petty made a lasting impression on Detroit manufacturers. In a Detroit fairgrounds race before a packed grandstand, Petty was involved in a spectacular crash that bent everything on his Dodge but the seat. He rolled over several times but still managed to finish the race. It was just such determination that was to lead Lee Petty to fifty-four career victories and a future in Grand National competition unmatched by men with less skill and ambition.

Lee Petty was the first stock car driver in history to win the coveted Grand National title three times. He won it first in 1954 in a Chrysler. He won it again four years later driving an Oldsmobile and became a repeat winner the following season driving an Oldsmobile and a Plymouth. Lee Petty never asked for an inch on a race track, nor did he give one. "Lee was a great competitor," says one longtime fan. "The only thing wrong with him was he thought he was supposed to win every race. Second place was for somebody else."

Petty's greatest year was 1959, even though he had won the championship three times by then. He entered forty-nine races, finished forty-one and was in the top five thirty-one times. He won twelve events that boosted his prize money for the season up to $45,570—the most earned by a driver for one season between 1950 and 1960. Lee, who in 1959 won the inaugural Daytona International Speedway event in a photo finish with Johnny Beauchamp, was also voted "Most Popular Driver" three consecutive years 1953, 1954 and 1955. His career as an active driver ended in 1961 at the scene of his biggest triumph. Once again battling Beauchamp for the lead, Petty's familiar blue No. 42 sailed over the guard rail to a crushing landing far below in a parking lot. Lee suffered a punctured lung, a badly broken leg and numerous lacerations. He recovered, which amazes doctors to this day, and even tried his hand at the wheel in a couple of races during the

NASCAR president Bill France offers Lee Petty congratulations after one of Petty's many Grand National victories.

Lee Petty's son Richard (right) *carried on the family racing tradition after his father retired from driving competition. Petty quickly became one of the sport's most successful drivers. Here he appears at the Pure-Darlington Record Club banquet with old pro Buck Baker* (left) *and former world middleweight champion Mickey (The Toy Bulldog) Walker.*

1962 season but, "It wasn't fun for me anymore," Lee says, "so I quit." When he retired from driving, Lee left the steering wheel in most capable hands, those belonging to his son, Richard.

It was Richard who finally broke his father's career record for Grand National victories when he captured his fifty-fifth win in the Rebel 400 at Darlington in 1967. Lee does not spend that much time involved with the Petty's present-day Plymouth racing operation. As Richard says, "We pretty much do what we want to, but when we get in trouble, the boss man is there to bail us out." Lee might say he lost his competitive urge behind the wheel of a stock car, but amateur golfers will say he didn't, he just transferred it from the cockpit to the first tee. Lee took up golf and within a year had managed to break 90. He is seldom over 75 or 80 now. "He plays golf just like he used to drive," says one Chrysler official who has known Petty for many, many years. "He never tees the ball up if he doesn't think he's supposed to win. He hasn't changed much."

Richard Petty has certainly followed in his father's footsteps. The youngster who for years accompanied his racing father to tracks all over the country took his dad's advice to heart "If you're going to do something, be the best at it." Few could argue with that when it comes to Richard Petty and stock car racing. He holds virtually every record in the sport, has won at virtually every track that ever held a NASCAR event, is a four-time national champion, a distinction which no other stock car driver shares, has won more races than any stock car driver in NASCAR history, has won more money than any stock car driver in history, has been voted NASCAR's "Most Popular Driver" with regularity, etc., etc. Richard Petty credits his tremendous success to a lot of hard work, a lot of good breaks and a crew that has been with him since his first race. Brother Maurice builds the engines for Richard's Plymouths, and cousin Dale Inman serves as the chassis expert. "We grew up together as kids the first time," says Richard. "Then we grew up together again as a stock car racing team."

Richard's career began at the ground level in his father's modest behind-the-house shop. "My first job was to sweep the floor," says

The familiar Petty blue Plymouth is the winningest car ever to hit the nation's stock car tracks, and No. 43 is a household numeral throughout the country. Richard Petty has won more stock car races than any driver in history.

Richard. "Daddy gradually let me do things like change the oil, that sort of thing." When Richard was twenty-one, he told Poppa Lee, "I want to drive a race car." Lee had known it was coming, so he pointed to one of the cars he himself had driven the year before. "Have at it, son," Lee Petty said. "That's about all he said," Richard recalls, "except to tell me I ought not drive it any faster than what felt good to me." Richard Petty's first Grand National race was a 100-miler in Columbia, South Carolina—he finished sixth. The young son of established star Lee Petty did not win in his first season and freely admits, "I didn't do very good at all that first year. In fact, I tore up a whole bunch of equipment before I learned what it was all about. I suspect if I had been driving for anyone else, I probably would have been looking for a ride."

Richard captured his first victory in his second season—back at the scene of his first race, Columbia. That season, 1959, Richard Petty was NASCAR's "Rookie of the Year." Petty's No. 43 soon became a household number. Little boys riding homemade soapbox racers down local hills painted their machines blue and splashed giant No. 43s all over them. By the end of 1964 Petty

The Petty Engineering pit crew is considered one of the finest in stock car racing. Members of the crew refuel Petty's car while one member hands the popular driver a cup of water (see long stick on right with rag draped across it). Petty usually drives with a wet rag dangling from his mouth. He says it keeps his mouth from drying out.

One of the most familiar pictures in sports sections is Petty in the winner's circle. Richard Petty has won major races at every southern superspeedway except Talladega, which was built in 1969.

was well on the way to becoming stock car racing's first millionaire. That season Richard won the Daytona 500 for his first superspeed-way victory. He also won almost $100,000 in prize money. Three years later Petty so dominated things that stock car fans began to bet on drivers to place and show, they automatically figured Petty would win. He captured twenty-seven Grand National victories in 1967, which is still the record for single-season wins. Richard topped the $1 million mark for prize money in 1971 in Atlanta. He has won at every superspeedway with the exception of Charlotte, his home-state track.

Petty suffered the worst wreck of his career at Darlington, scene of some of his greatest triumphs, including the 1966 and 1967 Rebel 400s and the Southern 500 of 1967. The Plymouth super-star who has refused to poor-mouth Darlington's slick, narrow surface over the years wiped out one car on the first day of time trials. His crew headed frantically for Randleman and returned with Richard's short-track Plymouth. He qualified and was running well when the hearts of some 70,000 stock car fans skipped a couple of beats. Richard's Plymouth crashed into the outer concrete wall at full speed, spun across the track and bashed into the inside concrete wall. The car then flipped violently down the straightaway, with helpless Richard dangling from his shoulder harness. However, he escaped with only a dislocated shoulder and later said, in typical Richard Petty candor, "I got a little behind in my steering."

If his driving abilities haven't been enough to satisfy Petty's loyal legions of fans (his popularity in racing is akin to that which Arnold Palmer enjoys in golf), Petty has complemented skill with an unmatched earthy personality. He maintains touch with his fans, always having time for autographs and a word or two. "Petty's head never has and never will outgrow his helmet," says one race promoter. Petty, by the end of the 1971 season, had won 130 Grand National events of a total 184 won by drivers of Plymouth stock cars. No wonder they call him Mr. Plymouth.

Of the fifty-four Grand National events won by Plymouth drivers other than Richard Petty, none has been more publicized than a race won by California's Johnny Mantz. Mantz drove a black No. 98 Plymouth to victory in the first superspeedway stock car race in history, the inaugural Southern 500 at Darlington in 1950. Mantz, a native of Long Beach, combined skill with planning in taking the first Labor Day classic. While others were burning off rubber almost faster than their pits could provide it, Mantz maintained a constant steady pace in a groove he found away from the guard rail on the flatter portion of the track. It took him 6 hours, 38 minutes and 40.26 seconds to register the biggest payday of his life, more than $10,000. It was Mantz's lone NASCAR Grand National victory because the handsome driver later lost an arm in a highway accident. Mantz never raced again after the tragic highway accident, but history records the Californian as the first winner of what was to become the granddaddy of all stock car racing as

ABOVE: *Jim Paschal, a veteran driver of more than fifteen years in Grand National competition, was the sentimental favorite of fans when he won his first big race in 1967 driving a Plymouth prepared by chief mechanic Bill Ellis of North Wilkesboro, North Carolina.*

LEFT: *Pete Hamilton, a former NASCAR Sportsman Division champion, headed south from Dedham, Massachusetts, in 1967. Three years later he drove a Richard Petty team Plymouth to three major victories, including the Daytona 500.*

years went by. Mantz's win also showed Plymouth owners that their driveway machines had power and durability to match any other make.

The biggest winner driving a Plymouth stock car other than the Pettys is Jim Paschal, one of the sport's longtime stars from High Point, North Carolina. Paschal won twenty-five Grand National events in a career that spanned more than twenty years. He twice

won the world's longest stock car race, Charlotte's World 600, once in a team car belonging to Richard Petty, and again in an independent Plymouth prepared by mechanic Bill Ellis of North Wilkesboro, North Carolina. Paschal was easygoing and drove the short tracks with a smoothness much akin to Sam Snead's golf swing. On each lap Paschal put his car on the same tire marks as the lap before. The Plymouth-driving star began his stock car career in 1947, driving modifieds and other short-track mounts. He won his first Grand National event in 1958 but Paschal, extremely quiet, had been in Grand National competition off and on for almost twenty years when he won his first superspeedway race.

An avid hunter and fisherman, Paschal also invested his earnings wisely and operates a farm and a construction business in his native High Point. Paschal's constant hunting and fishing companion, Benny Phillips, says the beauty of Paschal is not in his nerve and skill on the track but "his down-to-earth friendliness that is hidden by his desire to remain in the background among strangers. Paschal is so quiet and unassuming, half the people in High Point don't regard him as a racing star. They just regard him as Jim

OPPOSITE PAGE, FAR LEFT: *Richard Petty, stock car racing's all-time winner.*

OPPOSITE PAGE, RIGHT: *Current picture of Lee Petty, three-time champion and father of Richard Petty.*

LEFT: *Maurice Petty, brother of driver Richard, tunes the engines in the Plymouths driven to more victories than any other car.*

Paschal," says Phillips, adding, "I guess that's about the best thing a man could be respected for—just being himself." When not hunting, fishing or tending to his many business interests, Paschal is often a competitor on NASCAR's Grand American circuit for "Pony" cars (Mustangs, Camaros, etc). He is also a frequent winner in that division.

Paul Goldsmith earned a spot among Plymouth drivers in stock car racing with a cool, calculated approach to racing. The first Grand National event Goldsmith won was in a Pontiac in the last NASCAR-staged race on the old Daytona Beach road-and-beach course in 1958. However, stock car fans of the nation's superspeedways remember him best in a Ray Nichels Plymouth that ran near or up front until Goldsmith decided to quit driving in 1969. The Munster, Indiana, native came to NASCAR with excellent credentials, having won the United States Auto Club stock car title twice and having competed several times in the famed Indianapolis "500." He was also a three-time national motorcycle champion.

Goldsmith was noted for his coolness in the heat of competition. His biggest victory was the 1966 Carolina 500 at North Carolina

In 1970 Richard Petty (43) and Pete Hamilton (40) teamed up to domi-
nate the superspeedways in their winged Plymouth SuperBirds. They
each won three major races with Petty winning an additional fifteen
smaller races to finish fourth in the championship standings.

Motor Speedway when he completely blitzed his opposition. Typical of Mr. Cool's level head was his reaction following a spectacular
crash during the Atlanta 500 in 1965. Goldsmith's bright red
Plymouth blew a tire right between the first and second turns. The
car rammed into the guard rail and flipped over on its top, skidding
lazily along the high-banked second turn for several hundred feet
before stopping down on the apron. When fire crews and rescue
workers arrived Goldsmith was calmly removing his driving gloves
and inspecting the damage to his car. "The only thing hurt is my
feelings," he said. Small wonder they called him Mr. Cool, the
stock car driver with ice water running through his veins.

Goldsmith, in addition to racing all types of cars, is also an
accomplished pilot and co-owns an engine rebuilding plant in
Indiana. He is also a partner in an automotive and safety business
with Ray Nichels. Goldsmith won a total of nine Grand National
events before his retirement.

Friendly Jim Pardue of North Wilkesboro, North Carolina, was
on the verge of becoming a top-notch Plymouth star in 1964 when

he was killed in a test crash at Charlotte Motor Speedway. The lanky, cigar-chewing James Stewart lookalike won two Grand National events in a Plymouth before his death. Pardue was extremely popular among fellow drivers and spectators alike.

The most recent Plymouth-driving star came South from the unlikely hometown of Dedham, Massachusetts. Peter Goodwill Hamilton landed a ride in a Plymouth team car owned by superstar Richard Petty and promptly proved the Petty team made a wise choice. Hamilton's venture South, which he capped with victories in three of the circuit's biggest events in 1970, came about as a result of much planning on the part of the former national Sportsman champion who grew up the son of a college professor. The blond, rosy-cheeked youngster first appeared at Darlington for a tire test as a spectator in 1967. He walked the entire track, much in the same fashion fabled Ben Hogan, the immortal golfer, is known to have looked over courses. H. A. (Humpy) Wheeler said that day at Darlington, "He'll be a great stock car driver someday. He's willing to pay whatever price it takes, and that's actually what it costs—the willingness to pay the personal sacrificial price."

The following year Hamilton entered sixteen Grand National

The old and the new of stock car racing was graphically depicted during the 1968 Southern 500 parade when the Johnny Mantz Plymouth joined the festivities. First car ever to win a superspeedway race, the Mantz car stands in stark contrast to Richard Petty's famous No. 43 Plymouth which won the 1967 Southern 500.

events in an independent Ford. His potential was obvious, earning the Massachusetts native "Rookie of the Year" honors. The following season, when no Grand National rides were available, he drove a Camaro on the Grand American circuit under the sponsorship of Gene White, the Atlantan who also owns veteran Lloyd Ruby's Indianapolis cars. Hamilton won twelve of twenty-six Grand American events entered, enough to catch the eye of Petty. He signed as Petty's teammate for the 1970 season and won the Daytona 500 in his first outing. He won both 500-mile events at Alabama International Motor Speedway at Talladega and went on to earn $131,406 in sixteen races, finishing among the top ten in twelve of the sixteen events. He then hooked up with Cotton Owens for the 1971 season but failed to win an event.

3 THE CHEVROLET DRIVERS

Junior Johnson has been around for a few years. Folks knew him for driving stock cars. The portly mountain man from North Carolina made sure he was noticed. Johnson's homespun philosophy went something like, "If you drive a stock car, there's only one way you can never have to worry about keeping yourself a good ride. That's to put your car out front of everybody else and keep it there as long as it'll hold together." That's the way Junior Johnson drove. First in a Ford, then in a Pontiac. Anything he could get his powerful fingers on for short-track events anywhere.

But stock car fans remember Junior Johnson for his association with Chevrolet—the Junior Johnson Chevrolet. Junior won fifty races during a career that spanned nearly twenty years. Winning,

Junior Johnson is considered the most popular of all Chevrolet stock car drivers. The mountain native of North Carolina led the factory Ford team on a merry chase during the 1963 season, when Johnson's Chevrolet led every major race. His philosophy was to "win or blow it up."

however, was not the sole reason for Johnson's popularity. Junior drove the Chevrolet most remembered by Ford fans. It was a 1963 Chevy, white with a red competition stripe down its nose, and a bright red No. 3 shading its doors. It was a car that left Ford Motor Company quivering in its wake. It was Johnson's charging tactics during the 1963 season that prompted Chevy fans throughout the land to snicker. "Ford's spending millions of dollars chasing that one little ole Chevy," so they said. "And the only way they can catch it is for something on the car to break. Junior Johnson just drives off and leaves them standing wherever they run." Junior left them red-faced and embarrassed, with one Chevrolet that wouldn't be passed.

Therein lay Johnson's tremendous popularity. He figured he'd lost the race anytime he was getting a view of the back of another car. He rarely did. "The name of this business is to race," Junior once said. "Only way a man is doing that is running ahead of everybody. If the car don't have what it takes, then the driver's gotta do what he can to make up for it. You run up front—or through the fence *trying* to run up front." Junior met his share of timbers in his day. The board fences he occasionally knocked down were nothing compared to risks the Tarheel took during a youthful career on some of his home county's mountain back roads.

Johnson's racing credentials carried back to those boyhood days in, over, around and sometimes off the roads around his hometown near Ronda, North Carolina, which is near North Wilkesboro, which is tucked away in a valley north of Charlotte. Actually, Junior's mailing address was more akin to that of other colorful mountain characters. Junior slept and slopped hogs in Ingle Hollow, a few bends, straights and dead-man's curves up the road from Ronda.

They called him the "Wild Man from Ronda." There was the night in Columbia, South Carolina, when Johnson had a comfortable lead over the field, popped a tire coming off the fourth turn of the dusty dirt track and crashed through the wooden fence. The front end of the car was badly damaged, but Johnson drove it back out on the track. He tried to finish the race, but the car was overheating as a result of a damaged radiator. They called him the "Ronda Roadrunner." And they called him "the man even Ford Motor Company's millions can't catch." Whatever they called Junior Johnson, he drove as if to live up to the names. He drove with reckless abandon. Caution was something to toss to the wind —and to other drivers. Junior roared around the race track like a man hauling moonshine with a revenue agent fast on his heels. And, in Johnson's case, the dirt track "agents" never got close enough to bite. Johnson drove as if he was trying to outrun life. The popular legend surrounding his driving ability goes back to his younger days when he reportedly took on-the-job driver training behind the wheels of cars which revenue agents were forever trying to gain on. The competition, so the story goes, was much too tough for the federal men.

Johnson's fifty wins were spread over the years, but eight of them stand out to Chevy fans—the eight Grand National events he won in 1963. Junior did not simply outrun such drivers as Fireball Roberts, Fred Lorenzen, Richard Petty and the like, he outran one

LEFT: *Rex White, one of the smallest men ever to sit behind the wheel of a Grand National stock car, drove a Chevrolet to the championship in 1960.* RIGHT: *Alfred (Speedy) Thompson of Monroe, North Carolina, captured the 1955 Southern 500 at Darlington in a Chevrolet.*

of Detroit's leading makers of automobiles. Johnson and his independent Chevy, immaculately prepared by Daytona Beach chief mechanic Ray Fox, caused more cussing behind closed executive doors than any single stock car combination in history. It was Johnson and his Chevy versus Ford. The man with no money bucking the bank. Only Johnson won. Not every race, but enough to make Ford, Chrysler and independent owners seek his services under lucrative contracts. Had Johnson been a baseball player at the time, he could have made an agent enough money to retire following the 1963 season. "Ford wanted to get him under contract just so they wouldn't have to compete against him," says veteran stock car observer Mike Harkey of Columbia, South Carolina. "They just couldn't stand the thought of Junior outrunning them for another season."

Junior, a drawling conversationalist whose belly sprawls across his midsection in testimony to good, old-fashioned southern cooking, led every race he entered in 1963. Every race. His foot was hotter than the flame-colored numbers splashed across his Chevy's doors. He captured two major events, the Dixie 400 at Atlanta International Raceway and the National 400 at Charlotte Motor Speedway. But Junior blew the doors off everything in sight whether he won or not. As long as the engine and other parts of the Chevy could stand the heat, Junior blazed away at the front of the pack. He led, and eventually won, or watched the finish from the pit area after encountering mechanical problems.

Johnson's ability did not lie in his heavy foot alone. He was and still is considered one of the finest chassis tuners in stock car racing. He is also acknowledged as one of the best shade-tree Chevrolet power engineers to come down the mountain. Thomas (Fish) Vernon, one of the pioneer chief mechanics who prepared and maintained Chevies for Atlanta's Gene White in the middle Fifties, calls Johnson "the best Chevrolet engine man ever. He builds the best Chevrolet stock car racing engine in the business. If there's some way to spring one more horsepower out of an engine, Junior Johnson will find the way."

Never one to mince words, when Johnson hung up his helmet

Bobby Allison, one of the present-day's biggest stock car stars, earned the title as Chevrolet's "Mr. Independent" during the Sixties. He now drives Junior Johnson's Chevy, much to the delight of fans.

following the 1966 season the thirty-four-year-old star, a legend in his own day, said simply, "I've been driving so long, I've about lost interest in the driving part of it. They're running right on the ragged edge now, and I don't feel I can take the chances I took a year ago, or the year before. I'm getting too old to take the chances I used to take. I'd like to step aside and make way for some of these younger fellows." Chevrolet fans could never remember Johnson any other way. "If anyone ever took more chances, if anyone ever had a more daring style, if anyone ever thrilled stock car fans more than Junior Johnson," a racing veteran said recently, "I don't believe the fans could stand it." Johnson, whose retirement thoughts began when his friend and lifelong competitor Fireball Roberts died in 1963, became the crew chief of his own racing operation. And the Johnson cars have been winning ever since.

Johnson's competitor, the fabled Fireball Roberts, gave Chevy-lovers something to cheer about before he glued himself to the cockpit of a Pontiac. Roberts, with financial backing from Atlantan Frank Strickland, drove a year-old Chevrolet on the NASCAR Grand National circuit in 1958. Prepared by Paul McDuffie, the Chevrolet was driven to numerous victories by Roberts, but none was more impressive than the Southern 500 at Darlington. Roberts didn't just win it. He made a laugher out of it. Once Eddie Pagan, the pole winner, was eliminated by one of the most spectacular crashes in Darlington's history, Roberts breezed home a full five laps ahead of second-place finisher Buck Baker. "It was really amazing what Roberts did with that Chevrolet," says John Laux, one of Roberts' old racing buddies. "They blew everybody off that season. McDuffie and Bradley Dennis kept the car up for Fireball, and he just flat smoked everybody off. In a two-year-old car. It was like running a donkey in the Kentucky Derby with Eddie Arcaro in the saddle."

Chevrolet drivers combined for 124 victories from the 1949 through the 1972 stock car seasons with Junior Johnson, Fireball Roberts and Buck Baker leading the way. Buck Baker. Ex-bus driver. Fender bender. Nose buster. Competitor. What a competitor. Ford fans say Baker is really a Ford man at heart. Chevy fans

A pair of Fords and a Chevrolet had the front row positions for the start of the 1958 Southern 500. Eddie Pagan (right) *earned the pole in his Ford. Glenn (Fireball) Roberts was second fastest in his year-old Chevy and Little Joe Weatherly* (left) *was third. After Pagan crashed, Roberts waltzed home an easy winner.*

say the same thing. So do Chrysler fans. If Edsel Ford had wanted a successful car, he should have put Baker in its seat and headed him in the direction of the next Grand National race.

Baker won in everything, though he is chiefly remembered for his Chrysler-driving days under the Mercury Outboards banner of legendary Karl Kiekhaefer's famous racing team. Baker, however, won the Grand National title driving a 1957 Chevy during the 1957 season. Baker, Herb Thomas and Alfred (Speedy) Thompson combined to dominate most of the short-track events during the 1955–57 seasons. Thomas won the 1955 Southern 500 at Darlington in a Chevy, and Thompson repeated two years later. Prior to the 1955 season Chevrolet had not won a Grand National event.

Thompson, whose nickname matched his driving style, followed in the footsteps of his father and an older brother in crawling into the fast world of stock car competition. Speedy's name and driving style captured the fancy of many fans as he won a total of nineteen

Fireball Roberts waves to the crowd as he takes the checkered flag in the 1958 Southern 500 at the wheel of a 1957 Chevrolet.

Grand National events before quitting. His last big win, the National 400 at Charlotte Motor Speedway, was practically in his backyard. A native of Monroe, North Carolina, only a few miles from Charlotte, Thompson drove a Wood brothers-prepared Ford to victory in that event, but Chevy fans will quickly tell you it was "all driver." Chevy fans, as do Ford fans, heap credit on drivers when they're in the "other brand." It's the car for the most part, though, when drivers are in the same brand the fan drives to work every day.

Thompson's wins in a Chevrolet came against some of that make's greatest drivers of all time. Men like Roberts, Baker, Bob Welborn, Yankee Jim Reed (scourge of the short tracks), Johnny Beauchamp and Rex White. Thompson's Southern 500 win made headlines throughout the nation in 1957, because Speedy became the first driver in the history of the country's longest, richest stock car event to average better than 100 miles an hour for the grueling distance. His Chevrolet managed an average of 100.100 mph.

Bob Welborn, born in Atlanta, Georgia, won the NASCAR convertible championship three times before that division was abolished. He was one of the most colorful drivers of the pre-1960 period. The short, stocky driver is a part of the hundreds of off-track legends surrounding the middle years of the sport. One of those legends is that little Joe Weatherly bet Welborn he couldn't do a 180-degree turnaround on a narrow bridge in Florida. Without lifting the gas, of course. Legend has it Welborn accomplished the feat. He got a running start, sped onto the bridge, kept the throttle on the floorboard, tossed the car into a broadslide with the front bumper inches from the bridge rail on one side and the rear bumper within an eyelash on the other and came back without a scratch on the car. To make it even more difficult it was supposed to have been raining at the time. Welborn retired from competition with seven Grand National wins to his credit, most in Chevrolets.

Jim Reed captured a lot of national attention by winning the 1959 Southern 500 in a Chevrolet. Reed was the first native Yankee to win the premier southern event. The Peekskill, New York, native won it with ease, too—his Impala had a two-lap margin on runner-up Bob Burdick. That 1959 event also goes down in history as one of Chevrolet's finest hours on a superspeedway. Chevrolet grabbed five of the top ten spots with Bobby Johns third, Jim Paschal sixth, Larry Frank eighth and Buck Baker ninth, all in Chevies.

One of the biggest names in Chevrolet's stock car history was one of the smallest men ever to climb into the cockpit. Rex White didn't stand much taller than one of the gas cans used to refuel the thundering machines. The northern native who settled in Spartanburg, South Carolina, was only five feet four inches tall and weighed only 140 pounds. He looked as if he needed both feet to floorboard the gas pedal. Once races started, however, White proved size had nothing to do with driving the big stockers.

If it hadn't been for the little charger with the George Gobel looks, Chevrolet today would not have its name listed among the NASCAR season-point champions. White, winner of twenty-six

ABOVE: *Bob Welborn won NASCAR's convertible Grand National division three times in a Chevrolet. He also won seven Grand National races in the hard-top competition after NASCAR abolished the convertible circuit.*

LEFT: *Buck Baker stands beside his Chevrolet prior to qualifying at Daytona in 1959. Baker drove a Chevrolet to victory in the Southern 500 at Darlington in 1955. He has driven virtually every make of car in Grand National competition and also has won in virtually every make of car.*

Grand National events during his career, captured the 1960 Grand National championship at the wheel of a Chevy prepared by veteran mechanic Louie Clements. Rex drove the short tracks with reckless abandon and dominated the circuit in 1960. His biggest win, however, came two years later when he drove to victory in the Dixie 400 at Atlanta.

Chevrolet fans also lay claim to a pair of the sport's most colorful drivers never to win a Grand National event. George Green, a cigar-chewing army sergeant, developed many loyal followers with his constant desire to win an event, although he drove equipment much inferior to that of the better-known front-runners. And J. T. Putney, an airplane pilot by profession, captured the fans' hearts with his fearless determination to compete against the factory teams in a Chevrolet that came up short in horsepower and financing. Putney's flat-out style prompted fans to remark, "If he flies an airplane the way he drives a stock car, I don't know whether I want to get anywhere that fast or not."

One of Chevrolet's better-known drivers in recent years had to switch to Ford to have a big year at the pay window. Oh, how that makes Chevy fans smart. Bobby Allison, the Alabamian who became known in the late Sixties as Mr. Independent Chevy, landed the Holman-Moody Ford ride for the second half of the 1971 season and won practically everything in sight. He took Talladega, Darlington, Charlotte—you name it, Bobby Allison won it. But John Holman and Ralph Moody split after the 1971 season, and Bobby was looking for a ride. He didn't have to look far—Junior Johnson wanted someone to put in his Chevrolet. He looked no further than Allison, a veteran of more than ten

Former driver, now car owner/builder Junior Johnson gave Chevrolet fans something to cheer about when he showed up for the 1971 National 500 at Charlotte with two Monte Carlos. Charlie Glotzbach drove No. 3 to the pole position and dominated most of the race, but he was running in fifth place when the race was halted before the three-quarter mark due to rain. Glotzbach's teammate LeeRoy Yarbrough (98) started seventh but tire problems caused him to crash during the race.

years' racing experience who makes his home in Hueytown, Alabama.

Allison first gained national recognition with an outclassed, underpowered, outfinanced, shoestring Chevrolet when factory support from Chrysler and Ford filled the Grand National garage areas. Allison, a handsome, all-American type who likes milk and doesn't smoke or drink, tooled his little Chevrolet into contention at every superspeedway event prior to the 1970 season. The factory stars couldn't afford to take a breather in the corner because Allison would be within earshot. He completely scrambled Detroit's brains for a couple of seasons by dominating the short-track events in his Chevy. When he joined Johnson and his Chevy team to begin the 1972 season, longtime Chevy fans were quick to say, "Well, he's just getting back in the kind of car where he belongs. If he won $230,000 driving a Ford [which he did in 1971], he'll top that before he quits driving a Chevrolet tuned by Junior Johnson."

Chevy fans swore to it, and they were right. In 1972 Allison won ten races, over $260,000 in prize money, and finished second to Richard Petty for the national championship.

4 THE DODGE DRIVERS

→

David Pearson's black eyes squint into the high noon sun as the Piper 120 climbs into the sky over Savannah, Georgia. "Don't look now but your door's open," he says. An open door might not be so frightening when pulling away from a stoplight, but it can be mighty uncomfortable when looking down from 1,000 feet. Pearson thought it was funny. After all, he was sitting on the side of the cockpit where there is no door to open. Pearson is like that —a barrel of laughs. On another day a state patrolman leaned his hulking frame through the window of the car and asked, "May I see your license?" Who's to argue with a state patrolman asking for a license from the driver of a car that has just tripped the radar clocks at better than 90 miles an hour in a 55-mile-an-hour speed zone? This time, Pearson is sitting on the right side. His stocking feet are propped against the dashboard and he's mumbling, "Boy, am I glad you stopped us, officer! I've been trying to get him to slow down ever since we left Spartanburg."

David Pearson is like that. He has an amazing sense of humor. His raw wit could make money on the talk-show circuit, but Pearson chose legalized speed instead. "I never did like school too much," says the part-Cherokee Indian with a smile, "and I sure didn't like working in the cotton mill. I liked racing, so that's what I decided I'd do."

The Spartanburg, South Carolina, native took to driving modified stock cars during the late 1950s. He bounced over such race tracks as Greenwood, Gaffney and Newberry, South Carolina. Wherever they cranked an engine, David Pearson was there to sit behind the wheel. Any wheel. "When I first started, I drove just about anything I could get my hands on," he says—then adds, in his own way, "Course, I didn't always keep my hands on what it was I was driving."

Veteran Spartanburg fairgrounds promoter Joe Littlejohn, who also served as one of the founders of NASCAR, says Pearson was as "close to a natural race driver as any I've ever seen." And that, stock car racing enthusiasts, is where Dodge came in. Pearson's heavy foot and youthful personality made a bona fide contender out of Dodge stock cars. Remember Dodge? It was the car little old ladies drove to school and back. Performance was measured in speedometer mileage. If the old Dodge made it to market on Saturdays and Cousin Jane's on Sundays, it was worth its salt. Forget speed and other hot rod stuff. Prior to 1963 when an Owens named Cotton handpicked Pearson to drive his Dodge, the cars had won only twenty Grand National stock car races since the 1949 birth of NASCAR.

The only driver of note to achieve anything in a Dodge was Lee Petty, who won quite a few short-track events in the old hump-backed machines. Lee, of course, overshadowed whatever make car he was driving with a winning attitude and ability. As a Memphis, Tennessee, sportswriter pictured him on June 3, 1955, Petty

David Pearson, the popular Spartanburg, South Carolina, native, was Dodge's number one choice as driver when the factories jumped back into stock car racing in 1964. Pearson won the championship in a Dodge by winning fifteen Grand National events during the 1966 season.

was a "brawny young man with the look of eagles in his eyes—sun-stained and sinewy and tough." And, it was added, "the man to beat in a red ram Dodge." It was also Poppa Lee Petty who drove a Dodge to victory in the first Grand National stock car race ever held west of the Mississippi River. He dusted off a pair of Hudsons driven by hotshots Herb Thomas and Dick Rathmann to win a 100-mile race over the Louisiana State Fairgrounds tract at Shreveport in 1953.

Another old pro, Buck Baker, gave Dodge its first share of any prestige when he captured the 1956 Grand National title by splitting his driving time between a Chrysler and a Dodge. But it was Pearson, after he first set the Grand National establishment on its ear in the seat of a Pontiac, who became the first Dodge driver to stick with the make for any length of time in the modern, super-speedway era of racing stock cars.

Bobby Isaac and Harry Hyde, his chief mechanic, teamed up in 1968 and won the championship two years later for Dodge. Isaac's No. 71 K&K Insurance Dodge is among the most feared on the Grand National circuit.

Oh, there were publicity-type things that kept Dodge in the sports sections now and then such as Bob Osiecki's Dodge entry in the Southern 500 at Darlington in 1962. Osiecki, a master promoter, entered the car with Darel Dieringer as driver. The two brought along a goat as official mascot of the Dodge, which used a ram as its hood ornament to symbolize power and prestige and all else a car should be. The goat made more headlines than the car. Mechanics of rival cars were feeding the goat cans, papers, cups, etc., and thanking the Osiecki-Dieringer team for providing a garage area cleanup unit. "Just throw the old oilcans down on the ground," they would say in jest. "The Dodge goat will get them." Needless to say, it was the last appearance of the goat. And the car. And the team. Dieringer later became one of Mercury's all-time driving stars.

Cotton Owens, who was still driving a little in 1962, liked what he saw in the youngster from his hometown of Spartanburg. He liked his style. David Pearson had driven most of the superspeedway events in a Pontiac for Ray Fox. Before that he had been named "Rookie of the Year" following the 1960 season which he spent mostly in patched-up machines, entering twenty-two races and winning $5,030 in prize money.

"I never will forget the first time David Pearson came down to Daytona for a race at the big track," says Littlejohn, himself the first man ever to average more than 100 miles an hour for the mile run down the beach strip. "He didn't know what to do. He had never been on a big track before. Never even seen one. But he knew he could do it. And besides that, he wanted to win some of that money. Actually, he would have raced for nothing." And Pearson, looking back, says with his sarcastic humor, "Shoo-man. What do you mean? I *was* racing for nothing. That Littlejohn sho' never parted with a nickel." Though Pearson will seriously say that Littlejohn played quite a role in providing advice and a voice of experience when he first began Grand National racing. And, he'll also add, "I'll tell you one thing, the first time I saw Daytona it scared me—and I ain't scared of nothing." Which is one of Pearson's favorite expressions all the time.

Relatively unknown, other than being Rookie of the Year, Pearson charged the Grand National circuit in 1961 like a wild bull in a china shop. His driving techniques often left machines

Buddy Baker, currently driving the Petty team's Dodge, is considered one of the hardest-charging drivers ever to run Grand National events.

scattered around the track. "When they drop the green flag, the other drivers know Pearson is going to start racing right then and there. It never does enter his mind to sit back and see what happens. He wants to be up front fast. Sometimes it gets him in trouble," the late Little Joe Weatherly once said of the Spartanburg driver. Weatherly had good reason. Pearson had tried to pass Little Joe on the opening lap of the Atlanta 500 in 1961 and crashed, taking Weatherly with him. Pearson roared down into the third turn aiming to be running first when they crossed the start-finish line. He didn't make it.

"There was only one thing wrong," says Pearson with a smile, recalling the accident. "My car didn't want to go where I was aiming it. You might say I learned a lesson that day. You can't just think you know where a race car is going. You better know where it's going when you aim it. That was the first time I hit the wall hard on a superspeedway. I was sore for a week." David says the accident wasn't the worst part. "When I got back to Spartanburg from that race, all I heard on the radio for a week was the song 'Hello, Wall.' This disc jockey in Spartanburg must have dedicated that song to me at least fifteen times a day. Everywhere I went, people in town were asking me if I had heard my song lately. *My* song, they called it. Every time I hear that song now, it reminds me of hitting the wall, but I've hit a few more since that day in Atlanta."

Pearson came close to becoming the first Grand National driver in history to win races at all four major speedways that season. He won at Charlotte, Daytona and Atlanta (the second time around, when he kept his car off the wall). A win at Darlington would have given him stock car racing's equivalent of golf's Grand Slam or horse racing's Triple Crown. They called him "Little David, the Giant Killer" after his surprise victories on superspeedways against such established stars as Fireball Roberts, Weatherly and the rest.

The Cotton Owens-David Pearson Dodge team was formed prior to the 1963 season. The team didn't win a race, but people certainly knew they were there. And Pearson, typically, was laugh-

Former NASCAR president Bill France congratulates Buddy Baker after the Charlotte, North Carolina, native blazed around Alabama International Motor Speedway in 1970 to set a world's record for closed courses at 200.447 miles an hour. Baker's Dodge was the first stock car in history to clock more than 200 mph.

ing off the winless season as a get-acquainted year. "We're just figuring things out with the cars," he kept saying. Always adding, "Besides, I didn't need the money." Chrysler Corporation was backing the operation wholeheartedly, and by the end of the season drivers of other makes were beginning to feel the presence of Cotton Owens' Dodges. Texan Billy Wade from Houston had joined as Pearson's teammate, the two running a pair of white-topped Dodges.

Perhaps the team was best remembered in 1963 for a race in Atlanta, the Dixie 400 in August. Pearson and Wade challenged for the pole position but qualified back in the pack. However, the two machines astounded a crowd of some 300,000 by zipping past Junior Johnson's blazing Chevrolet to hold the lead at one stage in the race. Mechanical problems resulted from the wicked pace set by the two Dodges, but Pearson had proved his machine capable of running at the head of the field.

By the time Daytona's 1964 Speed Weeks rolled around, Cotton Owens had a "bomb" hidden beneath his Dodges' hoods. Along with other Chrysler-supported teams, Pearson's Dodge and that of teammate Jim Paschal were powered by the most controversial engine in NASCAR's history, the 426-cubic-inch Hemi. Suffice to say, the Chrysler Hemi turned the competition upside down in

Outspoken Charlie Glotzbach teamed up with former driving star Paul Goldsmith in a Dodge for several Grand National seasons.

Daytona. Pearson's Dodge, along with other cars powered by the engine, was much faster than Fords driven by Fireball Roberts, Fred Lorenzen and others.

Pearson's first appearance in his red and white bomb ended with the young Spartanburg driver twisted like a pretzel beneath the dashboard of his car. Pearson cut a tire coming off the fourth turn during the race and crashed into the concrete retaining wall. "I liked having all that power up to that point," he quipped afterward. "When I hit the wall, though, I was kinda wishing I wasn't going so fast." Pearson was uninjured except for bruises and he went on to win eight Grand National races while finishing in the top ten forty-two times in sixty-one races during the season.

The following year Pearson, as well as other Chrysler-backed drivers, spent his time watching from the sidelines. NASCAR ruled out the Hemi, and Chrysler pulled out, taking their top drivers and teams with them. It was, until the 1969 drivers' boycott of Talladega when that superspeedway opened, the most famous racing boycott of all time. Pearson ran a few races in the United States Auto Club, but the greater portion of his time was devoted to staying in condition. He worked out daily at the YMCA in Spartanburg and constantly wished something would be done to allow him to run Grand National events once again. "That's just

Cotton Owens, Mr. Dodge among mechanics, talks things over with his son, Donnie, during a race at Daytona.

Dodge chief mechanic Harry Hyde signals driver Bobby Isaac during a 500-mile race on a hot, muggy day.

my luck," he said. "I finally get something that'll run and something happens where I can't run it."

Pearson returned full-time to the circuit in 1966 when the ban on the Hemi was lifted. He won fifteen races and his first of three Grand National championships. It was Dodge's first title, with the exception of Buck Baker's combination Chrysler-Dodge championship. David switched to the Holman-Moody Ford in 1967 and won his first race in this car, the Rebel 400 at Darlington. He has since won two more Grand National titles, 1968 and 1969, and is now second only to Richard Petty in total career wins, with sixty victories to his credit.

The rugged Carolinian is also considered one of NASCAR's better road racers but has curtailed his driving activities the past few seasons. "When you're gone from home as much as I was for the better part of almost ten years, you get to where you want to stay home some," says David. "It's about time my boys got to know me." Pearson had always said his goal was to win a NASCAR championship ring for each of his sons. That accomplished, there appears to be little left for him to conquer.

While Pearson blazed his name into the minds of Dodge fans during the mid-Sixties, others were making names for themselves in machines no longer linked with little old ladies from Pine Ridge or Pasadena, LeeRoy Yarbrough won his first superspeedway race in a Dodge, the 1966 National 500 at Charlotte Motor Speedway. Yarbrough later gained worldwide fame driving a Ford and a Mercury, but the Columbia, South Carolina, racer will likely never forget the Dodge he turned into victory lane that cool Sunday afternoon at Charlotte.

Other drivers drove briefly on the Grand National circuit in Dodges, capturing the spotlight for the tingling moments of victory that come only after a superspeedway event. Sam McQuagg, prior to a death-defying Darlington crash in 1966, seemed destined to become one of Dodge's all-time stars. McQuagg won only one Grand National race during a two-year stint, but it was the 1966 Firecracker 400 at Daytona.

His crash at Darlington later that same year virtually ended his superspeedway career. Longtime Darlington patrons recall it as one of the worst in the history of the track. "I never will forget that crash," says Darlington native Billy Early, born within walking distance of the old track. "Sam came off the fourth turn and appeared to be in good shape, but somehow he got tapped into the outside wall. The next thing I knew, he was heading for the pit wall. Concrete flew like shrapnel when he hit and then his car started rolling down the track, flipping over and over sideways. When it finally stopped, Sam crawled out and ran over to the apron. He wasn't hurt, but that was the second time he had been involved in a bad wreck at Darlington." The other time, a few years before, McQuagg, a native of Columbus, Georgia, and Cale Yarborough were battling for position in the first turn when their two cars locked together and Yarborough's car sailed completely over the guard rail.

Another Dodge driver was equally spectacular at Darlington. So much so, they renamed the first turn "Press Box" in his honor. Earl Balmer tried to get into the Darlington press box during the 1966 Rebel 400. Balmer wouldn't have needed a seat—he was riding one of his own, a bright red Dodge that will never be forgotten by members of the press attending that race. Balmer's Dodge blew an engine just as he entered the turn. The car slid sideways, bounced up on top of the guard rail and ripped out more than 200 feet of steel posts and rails. The car looked as though it would flip beyond the retaining wall and land in the elevated press box. "Hell, I thought I was on fire or something," recalls High Point, North Carolina, sportswriter Benny Phillips. "A big piece of wood bounced off my head and gasoline drenched me. I remember when it was over, I told them I'd beat hell outta anybody if they lit a cigarette, providin' I was still around after they lit it. Luckily, nobody did."

Balmer was not injured but his car was demolished. The native of Floyds Knobs, Indiana, drove a Cotton Owens Dodge in many races but won only one Grand National. Built like an all-American fullback, Earl was extremely popular because of his frankness about the sport. However, he returned to Indiana after deciding his luck could not hold out on the Grand National circuit. It was a sad note indeed when he drove a Wood brothers Mercury in the Southern 500 but was forced to retire the car after repeatedly banging into the third-turn wall at high speed. Darlington officials have since built a new press box to replace the old one that was called Balmer's Box for several years.

Charging Charlie Glotzbach first caught the public's eye driving a Dodge a couple of years too old to be competitive. The way he drove the machine, it didn't show its age. Glotzbach, a native of Edwardsville, Indiana, also drove for Cotton Owens and won the 1968 National 500 at Charlotte. Charlie was as well-known for his outspoken attitude as his flat-out driving—he never held back on either the gas or the tongue.

Glotzbach had driven a few Grand National events in 1960 and 1961 but returned to the northern short tracks for more seasoning. When he returned, he was ready. Following a stint as Owens' driver, Charlie took over the wheel for Paul Goldsmith when Goldsmith retired from driving to become a car owner. Glotzbach won a qualifying race in Daytona and also won a 400-

Dick Joslin (71) drove a Dodge in several of Daytona's old beach-and-road races but never won.

mile event at Michigan International Speedway. Now he is back as Cotton Owens' driver and his tongue is still as sharp as his skill.

Prior to Darlington's Southern 500 in 1971, Glotzbach shocked the racing world by saying officials of the track were "trying to murder us." He did not say it to get headlines, he said it because he felt it was actually true. Darlington officials have long applied a slick substance to the track surface prior to races there to keep the surface from breaking up during a race. All drivers will privately admit the surface is dangerously slick after application of the substance known as "bear grease." Glotzbach just happened to use terms that caught everyone's eye. He is, actually, a rebel in that respect since he does not believe drivers should tailor their thoughts to what is always good for the sport. "The stuff they put on the track makes it so slick, it's just like legalized murder," Charlie said. Then he went out and raced on it as did all the others.

His attitude is akin to that of some aspiring politician who might say, "I know what I say might not help get something done about what I'm talking about but that doesn't mean I can't say it." Glotzbach reminds people of Junior Johnson the way he talks about things. He doesn't believe in wasting any words. And he doesn't mind telling it like he thinks it is. "Marvelously refreshing chap," the British would say.

Elzie Wylie Baker, Jr., spent the greater portion of an inherited stock car racing career looking at race tracks from the wrong side of the fence. The son of legendary Buck Baker never had a square deal in a race car until he crawled through the window of a Ray Fox Dodge for the first time in 1967. Big Buddy, a bear of a man, banged through enough boards on his way up to heartily discourage a lesser man. All Buddy wanted was a break. All he needed was a good piece of machinery. He spent eight years awaiting a chance. When it finally came, the Charlotte, North Carolina, native was ready. Baker broke in the Fox Dodge like the man who had written the book on charging. He made people think he got out of bed every morning running flat out and belly to the ground.

He won his first big Grand National race at Charlotte Motor Speedway in 1967, the National 500, and followed up at the same track the following year with a victory in the World 600. Baker calls his first win, before hometown fans, his greatest thrill in racing. However, Buddy brought back the most memories to longtime race fans by winning the Southern 500 in 1970. Poppa Buck won the famed Labor Day classic three times, 1953, 1960 and 1964. Buddy could remember being in victory lane before but it was always hanging on his daddy's shirt-sleeve. The Darlington victory was immensely satisfying for the big, personable guy who spent an apprenticeship trying to live up to one of the sport's greatest names.

"I could remember hanging over the fence at Darlington when I was too little to get in the pits," said Buddy after his Southern 500 win. "I guess all little boys dream of something like this happening to them." Buddy did more than dream. Just a few years before his Labor Day victory, he drove an outclassed Plymouth to a surprising finish among the top five. That day, as he climbed from the car, his hands bore telltale blisters. It was typical. Buddy Baker wore more than one layer of skin off his hands during his frustrating climb up stock car racing's ladder. "That car," said Darlington official J. K. Schipman afterward, "has to rank with the all-time ill-handling stock cars. Buddy wrestled that thing all day. He did a helluva job just keeping it between the fences." There was another year when Baker was forced to run the Southern 500 without brakes. That's almost like asking a high-dive expert to perform with no water in the pool. Baker finished among the top ten.

Once the thirty-one-year-old former high school football star got a seat in first-class equipment, he quickly became a favorite of fans whose sole interest in stock car racing rode with the guys up front. The younger Baker, besides capturing the admiration of fans for his throttle-stomping technique in the heat of competition, gathered international attention in 1970 when he became the first race driver in history to top 200 miles an hour over a closed course. Baker zipped around the Alabama International Motor Speedway at Talladega in a Ray Fox Dodge at an average speed of 200.447 mph. He was also a leading test driver for the Firestone Tire and Rubber Company before its withdrawal from Grand National competition.

Baker experienced several metal-bending, mind-twisting crashes that failed to hamper his enthusiasm for speed. He suffered a broken collarbone in a test crash at Daytona, and sustained multiple bruises in a head-on collision at Darlington. At Talladega in 1971, Buddy was leading the pack coming down the homestretch near the end of the Winston 500 when his engine blew. The Petty-built Dodge was immediately engulfed by flames. Baker spun the car around to extinguish the fire but suffered burns on his hands, shoulders and backside.

Less than six weeks later he was back in a car and ready for another try at the Southern 500. A few nights before the race, Baker discussed his accident with Chuck Blanchard on a local radio show. The wit Baker displayed during the broadcast has done nothing to take away from his popularity with fans. Blanchard explained to the audience that Baker had been burned in the

Talladega crash. "Buddy, they tell me you're a branded man at the moment," said Blanchard. Baker laughed and replied, "Yeah, it kind of hurts me where I sit." Blanchard snickered. "I guess you've got some burns on that portion of your anatomy the French call your derriere?" Baker broke up. "I don't know what the French call it," he said, "but it's the portion of a mule you look at while you're plowing." The likable Carolinian then drove to a third-place finish in the race, despite the pain and obvious discomfort from the burns that had not completely healed. It was typical of Baker's desire and skill behind the wheel of a competitive machine.

Bobby Isaac is another Grand National champion who has made his mark on the NASCAR circuit at the wheel of a Dodge. Hard-luck Bobby they called him. When Lady Luck tossed out her bouquets, Bobby Isaac caught one for second place. Born and raised near Catawba, North Carolina, Isaac went to work in a sawmill at an early age. By the time he was a teen-ager, Isaac had graduated to the cotton mill. When most kids are reaching the age to swing around flagpoles and leapfrog over fire hydrants, Bobby was working a swing shift and building a burning desire to race. "I used to sit on the side of this hill in the late afternoons near home," says Isaac, "and I'd watch all these sportsman cars heading for races on the weekends. I said to myself then I would someday be a race driver."

Bobby was a natural scrapper from the first day he swung his leg through the closed door of a sportsman race car. He drove hard and fought hard. He did nothing to other drivers he did not expect in return. Like the night in Columbia, South Carolina, that Isaac was the victim of a local hotshoe's fender-tapping trickery. The competitor drove down underneath Isaac in the corner, bumped him straight in the door and drove on by as Isaac's car disappeared over the high-banked turn. Boards and dust flew into the dimly lit corner. When everything had settled, Isaac came stalking over the bank, helmet in hand. His car was totally demolished. Stumps and splintered wooden boards were strewn for more than a quarter of a mile. The race was stopped to allow workers to clean up the

Buddy Baker (3) lost his brakes during the 1967 Southern 500 and could not avoid the spinning car of H. B. Bailey (36). Elmo Langley (64) happened along and was involved also. None of the drivers was injured.

debris. Isaac, helmet still in hand, strode down the middle of the race track to where the cars were stopped. When he reached the car responsible for his crash, he stopped and let fly with a punch through the window of the car. Officials quickly pulled him away.

It was not the first time temper took the place of better judgment in the racing life of Bobby Isaac. Former NASCAR executive manager Pat Purcell, an old Irishman with a fighting disposition himself, loved Bobby Isaac. He once said, "Isaac keeps me busy by himself. He loses his license more often than he loses races. I take it away one day and he talks me into giving it back the next. But he's got to learn to control that temper the same way he knows how to control a race car."

Isaac drove the sportsman circuit like a man with just a few

Darlington, the oldest of the superspeedways, was unkind to Buddy Baker during his young days as a driver. In this race Baker's machine spun in the corner and crashed into the infield retaining wall. Baker kept at it and won the Southern 500 in 1970 at the wheel of a Dodge.

years of earning ability remaining. If there was a race every night, Isaac was in it. At one time he raced Wednesday, Thursday, Friday and Saturday nights, and twice on Sunday. "I couldn't find a track open on Monday and Tuesday nights," he said. "But I did run twice a lot on Sundays. Once in the afternoon and once at night. And if you didn't finish in the top three in just about every race, you couldn't make any money."

Isaac landed a Grand National car for one race in 1961. He lasted three miles and earned $50 for the effort. He returned to Grand National competition two years later in Daytona Beach. Bobby's 1963 season was spent in a Ford, but it was not until the southern-born driver headed North the following season that he landed a top-notch ride. Isaac spent the winter of 1963–64 in the cold shops of Highland, Indiana, car builder Ray Nichels.

It was the break Isaac needed to prove himself capable of handling a first-class ride, but Bobby did not necessarily enjoy spending the cold winter away from his native southland. In fact, he disliked that winter with a passion. However, he did like the Nichels Dodge he drove in 1964. He won his first Grand National race, a 100-mile qualifying event at Daytona. It was during the 1964 season that Isaac picked up the hard-luck nickname. He couldn't win for finishing second. He was second in Atlanta. Second in Daytona. And, if his luck wasn't bad enough during the 1964 season, it was compounded the following season when Chrysler announced its intentions of pulling out of NASCAR competition over the controversial ruling barring Chrysler's Hemi engine. "It took me ten years to get a factory ride, and they pull out of racing after one season," he said.

Isaac bounced from ride to ride for a couple of seasons, eventually hooking up with former USAC chief mechanic Harry Hyde for the 1968 season. 'That's the best thing that ever happened to me," Isaac says today, and for good reason. He drove the Harry Hyde-prepared Dodge, owned by insurance magnate Nord Krauskopf, to only three victories, but the wiry little guy from Catawba finished thirty-five of forty-nine races in the top ten positions. It was Isaac's best financial season. He earned $44,530. Owner Krauskopf was more than pleased with the results of his new team's first full season—Isaac was runner-up in the championship point chase. "Our goal," he said, "is to win the Grand National championship within five years."

Isaac came close in 1969, winning seventeen Grand National events and more than $80,000 in prize money. Once again, though, as in so many past years, Isaac's chase for Number 1 ended on a sour note. The following season, however, belonged to the Isaac-driven Dodge. He won the championship with eleven victories, finishing thirty-two of forty-seven events in the top five positions.

Isaac's burnt orange No. 71 became a familiar favorite with Dodge fans throughout the nation. Much more subdued in his temperament now, Bobby feels he must win the championship again. He doesn't worry about having to go back to the sawmill or the cotton mill anymore. But the fiery desire that got him out of that work still boots him around the tracks, looking for more than second place.

5 THE OLDSMOBILE DRIVERS

———————————————————————→

Truman Fontello (Fonty) Flock may have had wheels on his first baby bottle. After all, eating was probably no fun for the son of a former cycle racing champion without a little racing involved. Fonty Flock, the middle son of stock car racing's Fabulous Flocks, might have uttered something like this as his first words: "There are two things I want to do while I'm alive. I want to have fun and I want to race stock cars." His family obliged by building him a soapbox racer for his fifth birthday.

Thanks to drivers like Fonty Flock, old-line Oldsmobile employees can remember happy days when it comes to stock car racing. The Alabama native drove other makes during his twenty-plus-year career, but hard-core stock car fans remember the

Old pro Buck Baker poses with his 1953 Oldsmobile after winning the 1953 Southern 500 at Darlington. Oldsmobiles collected eighty-seven Grand National victories with drivers like Baker at the wheel.

mustachioed member of the Flocks flashing his victory grin through the window of an Oldsmobile 88. During Oldsmobile's stock car racing heyday of 1949, 1950 and 1951, Fonty Flock was perhaps the best-known driver in racing. If he didn't win, Fonty made fun of the loss. Fonty always made headlines. "They never made a race Fonty Flock wanted to lose," says Alf Knight, "but they never made a race he couldn't find something to laugh about, either. He was always the same, win or lose. You could always count on Fonty Flock to throw a little fun into a race. Promoters probably liked Fonty better than any driver back in those days."

Now don't get the idea Fonty didn't take his stock car racing seriously. He certainly did. Fonty won nineteen Grand National races during his career. Records of races in the early 1950s fail to indicate where the Flying Flock named Fonty ever backed into a win. Quite the contrary. He could have won many more, but

96

Fonty's equipment didn't always match his enthusiasm.

By the time NASCAR was formed Fonty Flock had been racing for a number of years. Bill Tuthill, head of Daytona's Museum of Speed, remembers Fonty winning the first stock car race ever held on a midget-type race track. He drove to a convincing win in that first short-track event on October 26, 1947, at Lonsdale, Rhode Island. NASCAR simply provided him with the opportunity to win more races, at more regular intervals, for more money. Fonty was one of few stock car drivers who claimed to make more than $10,000 a year and raced like it. Most of his Grand National wins were registered when Oldsmobile's advertising department was enticing stock car buyers to buy and fly the Olds 88 to the moon. Fans of Fonty Flock and other Oldsmobile drivers argued over such possibilities.

Everything was not always peaches and cream for Fonty Flock,

Buck Baker (upper right) *and Fonty Flock* (lower right) *gave Oldsmobile back-to-back Southern 500 wins at Darlington in 1952 and 1953. The Oldsmobile victories followed Johnny Mantz's* (upper left) *inaugural win in a Plymouth and Herb Thomas'* (lower left) *Hudson victory of 1951. Darlington's famed third turn provides the backdrop for the famous drivers.*

though. He turned over once at Daytona Beach and was six months in the hospital for a dislocated shoulder, a punctured kidney and multiple bruises. Fonty, however, found humor in racing's bad side. Fans loved such Fontyisms as, "I reckon I've raced on fifty different tracks in fifty different cars. And I suspect I've turned over at least once in all of them."

Oldsmobile's mark in the NASCAR record books shows a total of eighty-seven Grand National wins, and Fonty Flock drove the Olds 88 to its first headline-grabbing victory. Fonty shocked the experts who had gathered for the 1952 Southern 500 by wheeling his Oldsmobile home well ahead of the factory-sponsored Hudsons driven by Johnny Patterson, Herb Thomas, Bub King and youngster Banjo Matthews. It was one of only three races Oldsmobile won during the 1952 season. Fonty also won a short-track event at Hillsboro, North Carolina.

By the end of the 1952 season, Fonty's name was a household word in the heartland of stock car racing. However, Lady Luck kept slapping his Oldsmobile on its mechanical snout. "Even in 1953," says one old-timer, "Fonty easily proved he was the hottest thing in the 160-miler at the old Daytona beach-and-road race. He led all but two laps—the last two. He ran out of gas on the next to last lap after leading all the way. He still finished second." Fonty almost scored back-to-back victories at Darlington's famed Southern 500 when he finished only twenty-four seconds behind 1953 winner Buck Baker, who drove an Olds 88. Fans were angry at Fonty for switching from Olds to Hudson. The 1951 season was Fonty's best in the Oldsmobile owned by Atlanta businessman Frank Christian and maintained by mechanic Buckshot Morris. He won eight Grand National races and left a trail of track records throughout the country. He also kept fans howling with his antics. He once appeared at Darlington wearing a pair of Bermuda shorts when such fashion was considered totally sissy by a majority of those with whom he shared Gasoline Alley. Fonty also turned up in the Darlington pits with a monkey during time trials. "If I make a mistake during qualifying and everybody says you guys are mak-

Four of the fastest stock car drivers of the early 1950s get together prior to a race at Atlanta's Lakewood Speedway in 1953. Left to right: Dick Rathmann, Hudson; Buck Baker and Fonty Flock, Oldsmobile; and Hudson Hornet sensation Herb Thomas.

ing a monkey out of me, I'll simply have something to prove it by," he said with a lopsided grin.

While the likable Flock was making fans for himself and Oldsmobile, other drivers were doing the same in the record-breaking stock car which dominated the NASCAR circuit for three years. Of nine Grand National events run the first year of competition, an Olds parked in victory lane six times, with first-year champion Red Byron accounting for a pair of wins and Fonty Flock another two. Byron led a 1-2-3 Oldsmobile sweep of the Daytona beach-and-road race in 1949. Tim Flock, Fonty's younger brother, was second and flamboyant Frank Mundy third.

The first Southern 500 at Darlington in 1950 was dominated by Oldsmobile, with Wally Campbell of Trenton, New Jersey, on the pole in Oldsmobile No. 4. Seventy-five cars started the opening race and more than twice as many Oldsmobiles earned starting positions as any other make car.

The legendary Curtis Turner drove Oldsmobile to four victories in 1950. Another driver who was to later gain international fame in a stock car, Glenn (Fireball) Roberts, won a 1950 Grand National driving an Olds. Dick Linder, Fonty Flock and Bill Rexford added wins to give Olds ten victories in nineteen Grand National events for the season. Rexford, a gutty little competitor from Conewango Valley, New York, was also named the Grand National champion in 1950.

Never has one make of car been as dominant as Oldsmobile in Darlington's first Southern 500 on Labor Day, 1950. Well over twice as many Oldsmobiles qualified for the grueling inaugural race over the nation's first superspeedway as any other make. Oldsmobile was not at Darlington in number alone that first year. There was quality in the quantity. Wally Campbell of Trenton, New Jersey, set fastest qualifying time in his Olds with an average speed of 82.35 miles an hour for the eight-lap run over the then 1¼-mile track. Three-time Southern 500 winner Herb Thomas was also in an Oldsmobile that year as well as many other "name" drivers such as Roberts, Buck Baker, Fonty and Tim Flock, Turner, Gober Sosebee, and Hershell McGriff. Roberts finished second behind the Johnny Mantz-driven Plymouth after encountering tire problems throughout the long, hot afternoon. "There wasn't any doubt that the Oldsmobiles were the fastest things at Darlington that first year," Turner once said, "but nobody could figure a way to get them around that track without tires. They were blowing like firecrackers that day."

McGriff, a popular native of Portland, Oregon, finished third in the Southern 500 the following year at Darlington. Fonty Flock grabbed the next one, and Charlotte's Buck Baker made it two in a row for Oldsmobile the following year. It was Baker's first of three Southern 500 wins in three different makes of cars.

McGriff, the Pacific Northwest stock car champion, won four Grand National races in an Oldsmobile. The 1950 Mexican road race champion and another Portland native, Bill Amick, represented the Far West admirably on their cross-country treks seeking fame and competition. "That Hershell McGriff was some kind of race driver," recalls one veteran NASCAR promoter. "He didn't run but a few races the first year he came East, but he looked pretty good. The second year he came down here to race, he put the regular southern drivers to work. And he was as nice a fella as you'd ever hope to meet."

Colorful Fonty Flock (left) *jokes with younger brother Tim prior to a Grand National event in 1955. Fonty once drove an Oldsmobile at Darlington wearing Bermuda shorts. The rebel hat he is wearing in this picture was given to him by Darlington International Raceway president Bob Colvin.*

Oldsmobile's final moment in the national limelight came in 1954. Five of the first six qualifying spots at Darlington belonged to Oldsmobiles. Buck Baker was on the pole at 108.261, Fireball Roberts was second fastest, McGriff was third, Eddie Skinner fourth and Amick, McGriff's Oregon neighbor, sixth. But Herb Thomas and his honking Hudson won. It was to be Oldsmobile's last chance at a big one. Turner, who qualified in seventeenth position, led more than 200 laps of the 364-lap grind but could not run down Thomas at the finish.

The better drivers switched to other makes following the 1954 season and only Lee Petty, the North Carolinian with a knack for winning, attempted to make a contender of Oldsmobile machines in later years. Petty qualified an Oldsmobile in ninth starting position for the 1958 Rebel 300 at Darlington, but folks were whispering that if it weren't for the old pro, "his Oldsmobile wouldn't be competitive." Certainly, the days of the old "Rocket Oldsmobile" were numbered in Grand National circles, but Lee Petty added yet another major victory to its asphalt battle ribbons.

He won the Grand National championship in 1958 and 1959, partially on the strength of seven Grand National wins in 1958 and five more in 1959. Oldsmobile fans, however, like to remember that last big one, the first annual Daytona 500 on the mammoth, 2½-mile track nursed to life by NASCAR president Bill France. Petty, in an Olds, won the inaugural event in a stirring photo finish with Johnny Beauchamp. An Oldsmobile has not won a Grand National race since that 1959 season and, in fact, has not fielded a competitive Grand National effort since. Still, many pioneer stock car fans will never forget the days of the Olds. The late failures cannot tarnish the glitter of the early successes. "It was really something when it was running," recalled Mack Evens, a native of Charleston, South Carolina, and longtime stock car racing observer. "Man, I remember when those Olds 88s passed everything else like they were standing still."

Eventually, it was the other way around.

6 THE HUDSON DRIVERS

————————————————————————————————→

Mention a Hudson in New York, and you're talking about a river. Say it in the South, and they may think you're mispronouncing that old, revered Alabama football name—Hutson. Hold on there, Harry. How about the car? The car? A Hudson? It was the hottest thing in NASCAR at one time. Check the record book. Herb Thomas drove a Hudson. So did Tim, Fonty and Bob Flock. So did Marshall Teague, the man responsible for the great Fireball Roberts' interest in auto racing. And how about Dick Rathmann? And Buddy Shuman, one of the members of stock car racing's Hall of Fame.

"I remember the Hudsons better than any other car," many twenty-year stock car fans might recall. Who wouldn't? Hudson

The late Marshall Teague, one of the drivers who gave Hudson Motor Company its brief but dominating run on the stock car circuit in the early 1950s. The Daytona Beach charger, the idol of Fireball Roberts, also helped that native of Daytona start one of stock car racing's most illustrious careers.

was unique in several engineering aspects. For one, the step-down interior design. Doormen at fashionable hotels in the country during the period from 1949 through 1953 didn't worry about people missing the step off the sidewalk, they worried about the Hudsons picking up passengers. "Step down, please," they said, opening the doors. They might also have added, "Hurry up." Hudsons driven by the likes of Thomas, the Flock boys and others were not known for waiting. They were known for racing, and the Hudson was the first make of American car to receive full factory sponsorship.

As Joe Weatherly might have put it, "Pops, it was flat-out factory support when those cats were driving them bullet-looking things." They were called Hudson Hornets, and they stung the competition for three consecutive Grand National championships in the National Association of Stock Car Auto Racing. Herb Thomas, a former sawmill operator from Olivia, North Carolina, grabbed the title in 1951 and 1953. In between, Tim Flock, the youngest of the racing brothers, earned the 1952 Grand National championship. Hudsons were driven in Grand National competition for only seven years, but records point out the speedy old Hornet could get the job done. Hudsons won 79 of 221 Grand National events before being swallowed up in a corporate merger with Nash.

Dick Rathmann, who came East from California to run the stock cars, grabbed thirteen Grand National races before hanging up his helmet. Typical of the type of driver who handled the controls of the old Hornets, Rathmann earned the admiration and respect of race fans throughout the nation when he won a 250-lap event at Oakland, California, in 1953. It was far from a routine win. His drive to victory before a screaming crowd of 8,500 spectators actually began four days and 2,500 miles before the checkered flag fell.

Rathmann, a gutty competitor, picked up a new Hudson along with chief mechanic Jim Ellis in Atlanta, Georgia, four days

Al Keller of Greenacres, Florida, hits the north turn on the old beach-and-road course in the 1954 Daytona 500. Keller was one of the host of drivers who made Hudson a name to remember for stock car fans in the early 1950s.

before the Oakland race and headed West. It was a wagon train journey with little or no sleep. "There's no rule in racing that says you've got to have sleep," Rathmann said later, although wishing such a rule might have been. Rathmann, whose brother Jim would later win the famed Indianapolis "500" with the same type of determined attitude, took turns at the wheel of the tow car with Ellis. A snowstorm was among the obstacles they encountered en route to California.

A hundred miles from Oakland, the tow car broke down. Rathmann and Ellis decided to use the race car as the tow car, arriving in Oakland, finally, at 1 A.M. the morning of the race. They immediately began working on the race car. "I must have drunk hundreds of gallons of coffee," said Rathmann. When time trials began at noon, Rathmann and Ellis were still working on the new Hudson. When Rathmann's qualifying turn came, the gas tank fell off. "It was weakened by the strain of towing the tow car for more than a hundred miles," said Rathmann, knowing full well the possibility of a replacement was unlikely. Apparently his long, pressing journey would end on a sour note.

However, another brand-new Hudson, just like Rathmann's, crashed during qualifying runs. Everything on the car was bent or broken—everything, that is, except the gas tank. Ellis immediately borrowed the gas tank from the crashed car, and Rathmann earned the last qualifying spot in the field. The crowd, knowing of his long journey and bad luck, went wild when Rathmann roared from the rear of the starting field to the front on the half-mile dirt track. He passed car after car, tossing the Hudson Hornet broadside in the turns with reckless abandon. It took him two hours and twenty-seven minutes to win the 250-lap event. Rathmann laughed afterward and said it really took almost a week.

Hudson's participation in stock car racing occurred during the days when all it took to become a stock car driver was a car, a helmet of some sort, a mean-looking jacket, a pair of boots and a big drink of hard liquor, white lightning if available. "A guy would get away with whatever he could back in those days," says pioneer promoter Joe Littlejohn. "They knocked each other all over the

Lining up for the parade lap on the beach backstretch of Daytona's beach-and-road course. The pack was full of Hudsons in the early 1950s, before Daytona's racing moved inland to the present superspeedway.

race track. If a fellow would let you knock him all over the race track during practice, that'd be one less car you had to worry about once the race started."

Herb Thomas and Tim Flock, a pair of the best bumper-busters in stock car racing history, accounted for seventeen of twenty-seven Hudson victories during the 1952 season. The twenty-seven Hornet wins stood as a record by one make of car until Ford drivers matched it in 1957 with full factory support. Hudsons driven by Thomas, the old North Carolinian with a Tobacco Road background, and Flock, whose family name carried a racing edge, completely dominated the scene, but it was Thomas who gave Hudson its biggest victories. Twice, the Tarheel Hudson driver won the Southern 500 at Darlington, 1951 and 1954, and after Hudson was out of the picture, the pedal-pusher from the Carolina sandhills won it again, in 1955, in a Chevrolet.

Thomas not only set records on the track in the Hudson. He also set a record or two in the pits as a result of fast work by crew chief Henry (Smokey) Yunick of Daytona Beach, Florida. Smokey, who long ago claimed to be the "best damned mechanic in town," prepared the Hudsons driven by Herb Thomas but actually gained more fame for his latter-day Chevrolet efforts. Smokey is perhaps best remembered by old-timers for a 1957 Southern 500 pit stop on the car driven by Curtis Turner. Turner's Ford was running hot, on the track and in the pits. Smokey changed radiators on the smoldering machine during a pit stop, and Turner returned to the egg-shaped oval to finish eleventh. Observers still claim it was the fastest radiator change in history.

For those modern-day mechanics who can't conceive of Hudson Motor Car Company meeting the demands of stock car racing competition, there is a 1952 Hudson publication that proclaims a clean sweep for Hudson, including Tim Flock, Buddy Shuman, Herb Thomas and Dick Rathmann: "Here is why America's foremost stock car drivers have switched to Hudson." That 1952 barrage of Detroit propaganda may have been the first employed in the Motor City to entice prospective car owners to buy on Monday what wins on Sunday.

Buddy Shuman went the full factory route. "As a stock car driver, I do my best to win races," he said. "I must have a car that will give me the utmost in engineering, safety and durability." Shuman didn't stop there, adding more for the Hudson house: "No

A Hudson Hornet leads out of the south turn of Daytona's old beach-and-road course during one of the 500-milers that headlined Speed Weeks on the ocean front. Hudson disappeared from the stock car scene after 1955, and Daytona racing moved to the paved superspeedway in 1959.

car in America can go around a turn like a Hudson." Shuman, however, won only one Grand National race before a hotel fire snuffed out his life. Rathmann, on the other hand, prefaced his remarks with the creed of a professional driver. "I can win more money and win more races with Hudson." Enough said. Thomas, Marshall Teague and Tim Flock were also featured in the "Huck the Hudson" campaign, but their actions proved much more meaningful on the race track.

Three Hudson Hornets were on the front row for the start at Darlington, South Carolina, in 1954. No. 14, on the inside, was Fonty Flock's car. The middle man, in No. 82, was Joe Eubanks, with Dick Rathmann on the outside in No. 120.

Flock was the factory favorite in 1952 by virtue of winning the Motor City Classic at the Detroit fairgrounds on June 29. Flock's machine led a 1-2-3 Hudson sweep before the hometown car builders who were thrilled due to the fact that none of the first twenty qualifying places in that particular event had belonged to Hudsons. Shuman was second and Thomas third. Thomas, however, was awarded the sportsmanship trophy after suffering tire problems thirty-five laps from the finish and losing two full laps. When his tires were changed, Thomas came back on the track and pressed Flock and Shuman the remaining distance. The fans loved it. The Hudson brass probably viewed it a little differently. They were probably wondering what the fool in No. 92 was trying to do. But Thomas' driving that particular day in Detroit was typical. As long as his engine was running, as long as the four wheels were rolling, Herb Thomas was going to try to win.

Flock, whose daddy raced bicycles and oldest brother Carl raced motorboats, combined with Thomas to win eighty-nine Grand National events. Thomas won forty-nine, Flock forty. The handsome Flock did more than his share to elevate the famous family name in racing circles. Before he quit, he established a string of consecutive wins and a record number of wins for one season that weren't broken until Richard Petty's fantastic 1967 season when the Plymouth star captured twenty-seven Grand National races.

Bob, the oldest of the Flock brothers to pick stock car racing as his sport and Hudson as his horse, won four Grand National races in a career cut short by a neck injury in a Daytona Beach accident. Sportswriter Terry Kay, who attended the oldest Flock boy's funeral in Atlanta, wrote afterward, "Bob Flock had a heavy foot

Herb Thomas, the North Carolinian who helped make Hudson one of the great car names in stock car racing history, was the last winner for the Hudson Motor Company team, taking a 150-lap race on West Palm Beach's half-mile dirt track in 1955.

and a love for keeping the pack behind." Joe Tompkins, an old friend of the Flocks, recalled an even more impressive aspect of Bob Flock. "The last time I was at Bob Flock's house," Tompkins said, "he introduced me to a little girl who was staying with them. She was from down in south Georgia somewhere. She needed an operation, and her parents couldn't afford it. Bob didn't even know her last name, he just told me she needed a break. He wanted to give her one."

It was Marshall Teague's impressive Hudson victories in Fireball Roberts' hometown of Daytona Beach, Florida, that sparked the racing desire in the youngster who later became one of the sport's greatest drivers. Teague, who let Roberts tag along with him around his Daytona shop, drove a Hornet to victory in the 1951 Daytona beach-and-road course event for Grand Nationals. The following year, Teague, a master of the surfside course, won the first race ever to be cut short by promoter Bill France. The race was scheduled for 200 miles, but strong winds forced an unusual tide, and France toured the course in a station wagon equipped with a public address system, informing pit crews the race would be cut short of the original distance.

With Teague leading the pack, just past the 100-mile mark, France announced the race would be terminated at 152 miles. The tide's irregular activity was forming water pockets on the beach portion of the course. Teague's crew wasn't sure if the Hudson could make the remaining distance without stopping for fuel. Teague didn't know either—his gas gauge wasn't working properly. Others in the race stopped for gas. Teague kept going. He feathered the Hudson through the corners and made it to the checkered flag but ran out of gas while touring the track on his safety lap.

Longtime NASCAR starter Johnny Bruner, Sr., will never forget that race. He was run over while waving the checkered flag. Tommy Thompson, involved in two spectacular slides earlier in the race, lost control of his Chrysler coming down the paved backstretch straightaway and dropped off into the soft sand on the shoulder. The sliding Chrysler careened into Bruner, knocking him ten feet in the air. He fortunately suffered only minor cuts and bruises.

Teague won seven Grand National events in Hudsons. He was killed at Daytona, February 11, 1959, when his streamlined Indy car crashed into the west turn wall after posting a lap of 171.821 miles an hour.

One of the most popular Hudson victories was the Southern 500 in 1951. Herb Thomas, after spinning out during the early stages of the race, charged back into contention to lead a 1-2 Hudson sweep of the second annual race that was to become one of the nation's most prestigious stock car events. Jesse James Taylor of Macon, Georgia, finished second to Thomas' Hudson in another Hornet. Taylor was later injured in a race at the Lakewood Speedway in Atlanta when his Hudson flipped violently. Taylor's injuries forced him to retire. Herb Thomas drove a Hudson to its last victory in a 100-miler at West Palm Beach Speedway in 1955. It was the last time stock car fans would see the old bullet-shaped, step-down machines in victory lane. However, from 1951 through 1954 the Hudson was a race car. Following the corporate merger with Nash, Hudson became just another car.

7 THE PONTIAC DRIVERS

———————————————————————————→

Perhaps no public protest has been more bitter. Certainly not in stock car racing history. Pontiac fans call it the day a stock car driver changed his name. Glenn (Fireball) Roberts, certainly one of the most talented stock car racers in modern-day history, suddenly became the "Benedict Arnold of Auto Racing." Roberts, you see, was Mr. Pontiac, king of the stock car racing road. Until he switched to Ford. Longtime fans of the great Fireball, fans who thought enough of the Pontiac driver's ability to tag offspring with his nickname, developed an overnight hate for the man many credit with giving stock car racing a much needed touch of class. Professionalism, courtyard lawyers might call it.

Glenn (Fireball) Roberts remembered a letter he received in

1962, when he switched to Ford from the cockpit of his trusted "Pony-Ack." "Dear Fireball," the letter began. "You dirty sonofabitch. You've made me the laughing stock of this town. I told everybody you'd never switch to a stinking Ford from your trusty Pontiac." Max Muhleman, a former sportswriter with the Charlotte *News* and one of Roberts' closest friends, says Roberts never quite understood how fans reacted as they did to the switch. "He didn't really have a choice," says Muhleman. "Factory support was out as far as Pontiac was concerned, and Ford's involvement was making it harder and harder for him to be competitive. And, after all, keeping Fireball in a car that wasn't competitive was like putting an all-star catcher behind the plate without a mitt. Or a home-run hitter at the plate without a bat."

Roberts, who drove his first stock car race in 1947 at North Wilkesboro, North Carolina, drove Fords, Chevrolets, Oldsmobiles, Hudsons—anything Detroit put together—during his career.

Glenn (Fireball) Roberts was perhaps the greatest stock car driver ever. Pontiac fans swore by the Daytona Beach charger. His Pontiac led every race he entered.

Pontiac driver Jack Smith (left) *checks lap times during practice with veteran G. C. Spencer. Smith was one of the most successful Pontiac drivers in Grand National racing history.*

However, Roberts and Pontiac, once he began driving the General Motors product, founded a marriage of speed and skill that made the name Fireball a household term throughout the South. No. 22. Black and gold. Prepared by the old master, Henry (Smokey) Yunick of Daytona Beach, where Roberts made his home.

Edward Glenn (Fireball) Roberts made his Pontiac a bathing beauty in a fast parade of horsepower dressed up in speed. As Jim Foster, the former Spartanburg, South Carolina, sports editor now serving as Daytona International Speedway's public relations manager, once wrote, "There, sir, is a racer. That No. 22. If you're in the infield near the pits, perhaps you've already noticed more than one mechanic whips out his stopwatch when that car starts cutting hot laps. But you can't really fully appreciate her until you see her from behind. There, friend, is the most looked-at rear end in stock car racing, including those wrapped up in bathing suits at Daytona Beach. You can guess who does the looking. The guys who drive the other cars."

Fireball Roberts made a habit of running his Pontiac faster than any other car. And any other driver. He held more qualifying marks with his Pontiac at one time than any driver in history. Everywhere Roberts and the Pontiac went, they went faster than anyone before them. Prior to the switch from Pontiac to Ford in 1963, Fireball Roberts was breaking Fireball Roberts' own records. If there was one thing Fireball couldn't stand, it was looking at cars through his windshield. He figured he wasn't doing his thing if he wasn't looking at the competition in the rearview mirror. Everyone else was supposed to be back there. Running second or worse.

Little Joe Weatherly, who drove a Pontiac for Bud Moore during one stretch of his career, entertains (left to right) *Cotton Owens, Fireball Roberts and Banjo Matthews with some garage-area humor.*

*Gene (Stick) Elliott (16) catches the full brunt of Emanuel Zervakis'
speeding machine during a Darlington crash.*

There is an unforgettable night that goes with the memory of
Fireball Roberts. The night was fragrant, almost blissful to the
well-known driver as he leaned back in the poolside chair at a
Florence, South Carolina, motel and savored the thrill of victory
once again. Earlier that day, Labor Day, 1963, Fireball had completed his second blitz of the classic Southern 500 field at nearby
Darlington International Raceway. There had been too much talk
of late about Roberts' retirement. People were whispering about a
loss of desire. They were saying he didn't have it anymore. When
questioned about all the gossip, Roberts, in a jovial victory mood,
became indignant and launched a verbal tirade. "I have no intentions of quitting," he said. "None. Why should I? There's more
money to be made in stock car racing than ever before. I won't
quit racing until I hit the bottom of the barrel."

Roberts never quit. He died a victim of one of the two things
he openly expressed fear of during his fabled career. Fireball died
as a result of burns he received the following year in a fiery crash

during the opening laps of the World 600 at Charlotte Motor Speedway. His machine spun on the backstretch at the 1½-mile superspeedway, flipped over on its top and backed into a concrete retaining wall. The car exploded upon impact with the wall. Fellow driver Ned Jarrett, also involved in the accident, was among the first to reach Roberts. "My God, Ned, help me. I'm on fire," Roberts cried.

Two months later, on the eve of the Daytona race he had won two years in a row, Glenn (Fireball) Roberts died. He died having won major races at every track except Charlotte. Roberts was the winner of inaugural events at Atlanta, Darlington and Daytona. He won the 1958 Southern 500 in a year-old Chevrolet and repeated in 1963 at the wheel of a Ford. His black and gold Pontiac was the Dixie 400 winner in 1960. He also won the 1962 Daytona 500 in the Pontiac. And the 1962 Firecracker 250. He drove his Ford to victory in the 1963 Firecracker race. A Fireball-driven Ford captured the 1957 Rebel 300 at Darlington for the old convertible division of NASCAR. Fireball drove a stock car the way he threw a baseball at the University of Florida—hard and fast. It was baseball, not racing, that gave him his nickname. "He really hummed it," says Darrell Simmons, a longtime observer of Florida athletics.

He hummed around the short-track circuit too. The youngster from Florida almost won the first big stock car race ever held, the Southern 500 at Darlington in 1950. Fireball finished second to winner Johnny Mantz. He was driving an Oldsmobile 88 with No. 82 painted on the stock-looking doors. Roberts' eventual number, 22, was being driven at the time by Red Byron, NASCAR's first champion. Little did race fans realize during that first big race that Fireball Roberts would create a legend with that number in years to come. He never won the Grand National championship, but Roberts became the first true champion of stock car fans screaming for speed. Roberts never went slow.

That night in 1950 in Darlington, Roberts traced his career. He talked about a long-standing fear of fire and a fear of getting in the lake at Daytona. He didn't like the thought of being trapped in

Race fans became accustomed to this sight. Glenn (Fireball) Roberts'
Pontiac leads Nelson Stacy's Ford through one of Darlington's turns
during the 1961 Southern 500. Roberts later gave way to Marvin Panch
in relief and Stacy went on to win the race.

a burning car or in a car under water. "He took his racing serious,"
says another of Fireball's closest friends, Gene White, who drove
against Roberts on the old convertible circuit. "Fireball always
concentrated on what he was at a race track to do. That was to go
faster than anyone else . . . and to win. Always to win."

Roberts, that warm summer night just a few miles from the scene
of his final triumph, discussed the differences between amateur
and professional race drivers. If Roberts had a pet peeve during
his heyday, it was guys putting on driving uniforms and helmets,
thus appointing themselves race drivers.

"There is one basic difference between an amateur and a professional race driver," said Roberts. "One real difference. Put up a race
track with a hard, 180-degree turn. Build it on a flat surface and
right in the middle of the turn, put in an escape road. Build it so
no one can get hurt if they try to make that corner too fast or make
a mistake. The amateurs will take that turn faster than profes-
sionals more often than not. So will the guy out of the grandstand.

They don't have anything to lose. Take the same type turn and build it on a cliff about a mile above the ground. Make it without an escape road. Make it tough. Make it so if the driver takes it too fast or makes a mistake, he's dead. The real pro will drive both turns at the same speed. That's why fans pay to see races. They know the guy in the car is risking his neck."

Fireball Roberts and his Pontiac cornered the market on running up front, but the Daytona Beach speedster had been there before. "People remember him for his Pontiac days because he stuck with Pontiac when nobody else did," says John Laux, a veteran Firestone racing representative now serving as team manager for Indy drivers Lloyd Ruby and Cale Yarborough. "But it was really amazing what Fireball did with that year-old Chevrolet in 1958. Man, they smoked everybody off."

Atlantan Frank Strickland provided the backing, and Paul McDuffie and a youngster named Bradley Dennis handled the tools for the Chevy. Roberts didn't just win the Southern 500 that season. He made a laugher out of it. Once Eddie Pagan, the pole winner, was eliminated by one of the most spectacular crashes in

Glenn (Fireball) Roberts ended his career driving a Ford but he kept the famed No. 22. He won the 1963 Southern 500 in the car, his last big win.

Darlington history, Fireball romped home a full five laps ahead of second-place finisher Buck Baker.

"And they set new track records on just about every short track in the country that season," says Laux. Which perhaps led to the spreading popularity of the Florida Fireball. He didn't have to win. People came to watch him go fast. Rarely did he disappoint them. He figured that's what bought his groceries. Roberts' familiar Pontiac in the early Sixties flowed around the race track like a powerful jet of steaming water, interrupted only by the currents of slower traffic.

"Fireball had the combination many drivers had not yet come to realize," says Laux, who once shared rooms with the stock car driver on the Grand National circuit. "He studied tracks like a student looking for a quick way out of school. He figured the more he knew about a track, the quicker he could master it. And he studied his equipment. He always knew what his equipment was capable of doing. He knew where he could go faster. He knew exactly where he was riding the ragged edge. He knew where and when he could pass somebody. And when he couldn't. He didn't rely on his foot alone. He used his head. And when the two got together, there wasn't a living soul who could touch him on the race track."

Laux recalls Roberts had a compelling desire to compete in the Indianapolis "500" on Memorial Day. "We were staying together at Indy in Sixty," recalls Laux, adding with a laugh, "he wasn't cheap or anything like that but he didn't throw away any money. Fireball was offered two or three different rides at Indy," says Laux, "but the complications that would have come out of it bothered him.

"We were resting in the room one night, and he said he didn't figure he could afford to run Indianapolis. He had talked with the United States Auto Club. They told him they'd be more than happy to have him. All he had to do was join USAC. That meant he faced plenty of potential trouble with NASCAR because the two sanctioning bodies weren't exactly hugging and kissing each other back in those days. If he joined USAC, he faced possible suspension from NASCAR. Or a penalty or something of the sort.

When rain interrupted the Atlanta 500 in 1962, Fireball Roberts' familiar black and gold No. 22 was leading and another Pontiac driven by Junior Johnson was second (3). Rex White's No. 4 Chevrolet is a few cars back in the pit road lineup.

There was no driver interchange at the time, and both sanctioning organizations were extremely jealous of each other."

Roberts decided he had too much to lose risking a switch. He figured he was making $45,000 or so a year driving stock cars in NASCAR. He knew the tracks and the competition. Roberts knew it would take him several years to become competitive at Indianapolis. He knew he'd have to have a top piece of equipment, and he knew he'd have to spend quite a bit of time learning the track. "Fireball could also see more and more superspeedways springing up in the South," says Laux. "He told me he knew the day was just around the corner when a stock car driver could make $100,000 in a single season with a little luck and a good machine. He forgot about Indy after that. I never heard him mention it again."

The man who was only thirty-three when he died did not confine his keen, investigative mind to speed alone. Fireball Roberts didn't look upon himself as a daredevil looking for a place to happen. He constantly worked with officials of the sport, thinking of safety improvements possibly useful within his profession. Roberts was one of the first drivers to come up with the idea of a race tire within a tire. An inner liner to prevent blowouts. The tire companies shrugged off the suggestion at the start. Roberts finally convinced Goodyear Tire and Rubber Company such an idea was feasible. Today, inner liners are required equipment for the Grand National machines. Roberts knew the prevention of blowouts would save many lives as well as a lot of expensive equipment.

Roberts earned many honors during his career, but two meant more to the Florida native than all the others put together. He was the first stock car driver to win the coveted Hickok award, presented on a monthly basis to the nation's outstanding professional athlete. Roberts was doubly thrilled when the sportswriters of his state voted him Florida's "Professional Athlete of the Year" in 1959 and later made him one of the inaugural members of Florida's Sports Hall of Fame.

Racing writers had long immortalized Fireball in print, but perhaps the greatest written praise he ever received came from an anti-racing writer, Jack Hairston, sports editor of the Jacksonville *Journal* when Roberts was inducted into the Florida Hall of Fame. Hairston had long put down stock car racing. "But when I met Roberts for the first time, I was sold on the man, if not the sport. He had as much class and poise as any athlete I've ever interviewed," Hairston said. "There's no doubt at all he belongs in Florida's Hall of Fame with all the other great sports figures in the state's history."

Typical of Roberts' entire career, events leading up to the 1963 Southern 500 cast him in the underdog's role. He had been forced to switch from his Pontiac to Ford the year before. Longtime Pontiac fans booed him for the move, which was considered to make him just another of the long line of drivers paid by Ford. Calculated insurance for Ford, some called it. Besides, Junior Johnson's Chevrolet was the hottest thing on wheels that year, with Fearless Freddie Lorenzen the favorite of Ford fans.

Roberts was practically a forgotten man when the track opened for practice, but his No. 22 was ready to challenge anyone for the

Popular Jack Smith made the No. 47 famous with one of the fastest Pontiacs in Grand National racing.

pole, as usual. Roberts took to the track, determined to dust off his rivals. The engine in his machine couldn't stand the pressure of Fireball's heavy foot. The tires screamed through the first turn above the press box, and the engine exploded, scattering oil and pieces beneath it. The car spun lazily in the shining oil and smacked the guard rail with the once-shapely rear end.

Roberts watched Johnson win the pole with an average speed of 133.414 miles an hour. Totally disgusted, he sat by while crew chief Jack Sullivan frantically replaced the destroyed engine. Lorenzen also qualified, as did six others. Roberts would have to wait another day.

Roberts, his Ford and crew were ready to take the track the following morning long before the dew in nearby meadows and cornfields had dried. He kept practicing. He kept getting faster. In the second day of time trials, Roberts posted the fastest time of the week. He not only turned the fastest single lap, he also topped Johnson's pole-winning average with a speed of 133.819 miles an hour.

Bobby Johns registered one of the most popular Pontiac victories when he drove home first in the 1961 Atlanta 500.

Race day was no different. Johnson fell out early trying to maintain a pace to keep Roberts behind him. Johnson's Chevy couldn't take the heat. That night, the man who had won his thirty-second Grand National event relaxed at poolside and declared he wouldn't quit until he reached the bottom of the barrel. It was only fitting he never dropped to that. Pontiac stock cars, "Pony-Acks," as fans called them, won sixty-nine Grand National events during a seven-year period of NASCAR's history stretching from 1957 and ending in 1963. In 1961 and 1962 alone, during the height of Fireball's Pontiac career, the General Motors machine captured fifty-two of those sixty-nine total wins.

Roberts did not win them all alone. Far from it. The 1961–62 results sheets for Grand National stock car racing read like a Who's Who in Pontiac stock car racing. Little Joe Weatherly was driving a Pontiac, along with Roberts, Johnson, David Pearson, Cotton Owens and Jack Smith.

Pearson, destined to team with Owens in later years to form an unforgettable Dodge team, had been named NASCAR's "Rookie of the Year" in 1960. He quickly earned the nickname of "Little David, the Giant Killer" by outrunning the more established stars in such major events as the World 600, Firecracker 400 and Dixie 400 at the wheel of Ray Fox's powerful Pontiac.

Owens, one of NASCAR's strongest competitors on the rugged modified circuit, was the scourge of the short tracks in his Pontiac, along with veteran Smith of Atlanta. Cotton Owens had been a stock car buff since watching races at the old Spartanburg, South Carolina, fairgrounds from a seat in a tree beyond the wooden fences. Owens won nine Grand National races, eight in Pontiacs.

Smith, on the other hand, captured twenty-one Grand National races. The handsome native of Sandy Springs, Georgia, is considered by most veteran observers of stock cars as one of the two or three best dirt track drivers in Grand National history. His record speaks for itself. Smith was rarely out of the top two or three finishing positions in dirt track events. He did not confine his talents to the short tracks, either. Smith powered his way to the front of many major speedway events, but mechanical problems plagued him constantly on the big tracks. Actually, Smith had the inaugural World 600 at Charlotte Motor Speedway sewed up with a multi-lap lead over the field when a piece of pavement tore a gaping hole in his oil pan, forcing him from contention.

Smith, still as personable as he was when driving the Pontiacs, retired following the 1963 season. He still is an occasional visitor to Grand National garage areas. As one young mechanic was heard to say in Daytona during Speed Weeks of 1972, "There's Jack Smith. Man, I remember when he used to drive a No. 47 Pontiac like nothing you ever saw."

Another popular Pontiac driver was Miami's Bobby Johns, winner of the 1961 Atlanta 500. Johns, son of former midget driver Socrates (Shorty) Johns, drove flat-out in his blue and white Pontiac. But since 1963 the days of the flat-out Pontiacs have disappeared on the Grand National stock car circuit.

8 THE CHRYSLER DRIVERS

————————————————————→

Don't laugh if someone tells you Chrysler stock cars were once the hottest cars in racing. It's true. The big, bulky, present-day luxury car of the Chrysler Corporation is a descendant of a line that once blew the fenders off Grand National competition.

With the youngest and most successful of the Fabulous Flock brothers at the wheel of a Chrysler, hopeful winners of Grand National races in 1955 and 1956 might just as well have packed their equipment and headed home. Tim Flock, the youngest of the racing family based in Atlanta, made a shambles of competition driving a Chrysler. So did other members of one of racing's immortal team efforts, the fabled Karl Kiekhaefer racing team. Chryslers owned and managed by the outboard motor king (Kiekhaefer started and owns the Mercury Marine Corporation) swept the competition off its wheels.

The hog-nosed, fin-tailed machines that looked more like something needed to bump noses with New York traffic zoomed around the speedways with authority. "Kiekhaefer's was the most organized team ever to get involved in racing when he decided to participate in 1955," says Hal Hamrick, a veteran stock car announcer who started a career of broadcasting a few years before Kiekhaefer's stock car racing venture. "When they came to the race tracks, it was for one thing," Hamrick says. "They came to win." Kiekhaefer was from the Vince Lombardi school of competitive thought: "Winning isn't everything. It's the only thing."

By the end of 1956 Chryslers had won 49 of 101 events during the 1955–56 Grand National seasons. Kiekhaefer's Chryslers won a majority of them. Lee Petty—who else?—won the 1954 championship in a Chrysler and also won several events the following two years, but the seasons belonged to the Kiekhaefer Chrysler team.

Young Flock started the 1955 season by winning the 160-mile

Buck Baker, one of stock car racing's all-time stars, signed on with Karl Kiekhaefer's Chrysler team in 1956. Kiekhaefer approached Baker and told him, "Mister, if you're as mean an SOB as everybody says you are, I want you to drive for me." Baker took him up on it and was one of the main reasons Kiekhaefer's team was so successful.

beach-and-road race in Daytona with Petty's Chrysler finishing second. It was an amazing victory considering Chrysler's strongest performance on a national level prior to that amounted to those short-track events won by Petty. Flock, who at thirty-one had begun to develop ulcers worrying about winning races, captured a record eighteen Grand National victories in 1955 while driving a Chrysler.

Of course, driving for Kiekhaefer was enough to give any mortal man a bad case of ulcers. Kiekhaefer was considered a wild man. A perfectionist. A driving, calculating genius who refused to accept anything less than a 110 per cent effort. Kiekhaefer attacked stock car racing with personal fury. He didn't expect to lose a single race. If his machines were running, he expected them to be running first. If he had three cars in an event, he figured they should be running 1-2-3. And it was not unusual for the Kiekhaefer Chryslers to finish races in just that order. In the first race of the 1956 Grand National season at Phoenix, Arizona, Buck Baker led a Kiekhaefer Chrysler sweep with Frank Mundy second and Tim Flock third. The best the competition could manage was fourth,

Karl Kiekhaefer's Chrysler team was impressive anywhere it raced, even if going in the wrong direction for a few brief moments.

and Kiekhaefer took pride in the fact that that car was a distant fourth.

Mundy, one of Kiekhaefer's team drivers during the Chrysler-dominated days, remembers well what it took to drive for the demanding Kiekhaefer. Mundy was a former AAA national champion when Kiekhaefer called, wanting him to drive a Chrysler in the Mexican road race.

"He was demanding," says Mundy, who now serves as sales manager for Kiekhaefer's Mercury outboards in the state of Georgia. "But he always gave the drivers the best of equipment. Nothing was too good when it came to equipment. What he didn't care about was hours. When he was wrapped up in stock car racing, he lost all track of time. He loved competition. And to me, he was a genius when it came to running a stock car racing operation. He was so far ahead of his time in thinking, that average people couldn't keep up with him."

Once he made up his mind to go racing, Kiekhaefer bought the Chrysler 300s and went after it tooth and nail. He hired the best drivers available—Tim Flock, Frank Mundy, Fonty Flock, Buck

Tim Flock's Chrysler (16) zooms down the Darling-ton straightaway during the 1955 Southern 500. Flock's bid for victory was stopped by mechanical problems.

Baker, Speedy Thompson, Jack Smith, Herb Thomas. Legend has it he hired Baker, the native of Charlotte, North Carolina, who was rapidly building a reputation as one of the sport's greatest competitors, with a conversation that went something like this: "Baker, if you're as big an SOB as everybody says you are, I want you to drive for me." Baker liked him and drove for him during the 1956 season.

Baker once said, as far as Kiekhaefer was concerned, "He took me out of the kitchen and put me in the dining room, changed my menu from hamburgers to steaks." Kiekhaefer went first-class. The prize money went to the drivers, except for 10 per cent that went to the mechanics. Kiekhaefer never took a nickel out of stock car racing. All he wanted was the personal satisfaction of whipping the factory efforts such as Ford's at the time. That he did.

"He called the factories the dinosaurs," recalls Mundy. "And, as an independent, he beat them at their own game. Everything was

132

a challenge to him. People either loved him or hated him," says Mundy. "But I don't believe anyone who ever drove for him really hated him. He made sure everyone who came in contact with him upgraded their standard of living."

Kiekhaefer's Chrysler stable so dominated the 1955–56 seasons, legend grew that he instructed his drivers as to which one he wanted to win. Those who drove for him scoff at the idea. "He didn't care who won, as long as it was one of his cars," says Mundy. "And he didn't care who finished second either, as long as it was one of his cars."

Alf Knight recalls promoting a 100-mile Grand National race in Columbia, South Carolina, in October of 1955. "I had already gone to bed the night before the race," recalls Knight. "About midnight the phone rang, it was Karl. He said he wanted to rent the race track. When I asked him when he wanted it, he said, 'Right now!' I went down and unlocked the gates and they ran till four or five o'clock in the morning. He didn't care what it took to win, he was willing to put forth the effort. Tim Flock won that race, too. Beat the factory Fords."

Kiekhaefer's competitive attitude carried over in everything he did. "I remember he hired the national water-ski champion one time to help him promote his outboard motors. He was loading the race cars for a race one time and the ski champion was standing there watching," says Knight. "Kiekhaefer looked over at him and asked him what he was doing. The champ indignantly told him he was the ski champion. Kiekhaefer told him that might be, but for the time being he was a truck driver. He made him drive one of the trucks to the race track. The ski champion waxed the race cars two or three times before the race besides," Knight added with a laugh.

"He bought a Ford one time just to try and whip the Ford factory team in their own car," recalls Mundy. "He did it, too. Buck Baker drove the car for him. After the race, Pete De Paolo, who was in charge of the factory Ford team, was kind of hanging around the car answering questions, and Mr. Kiekhaefer made sure he told people old Pete didn't have anything to do with the winning car.

Chic Morris, who developed a friendship with Buck Baker during his early days as a driver that has lasted until today, was in charge of all tires for the Kiekhaefer Chryslers. In those days, tires had to be broken in prior to races. Flexed, they called it. Morris handled the job and Mundy quickly admits the Kiekhaefer team never had a "flat as a result of Chic's work."

Morris, now a zone manager with an Atlanta office, fondly recalls his first meeting with one of the Kiekhaefer Chrysler stars, Buck Baker. It was at a bullring track in Pageland, South Carolina. As Morris told Bob Myers of the Charlotte, North Carolina, *News* a few years ago, "Baker won that race, probably the first and last they held at that old track. A car rolled through the fence into the crowd, and later in the race, another car rammed into the water wagon and knocked the people perched on its top all over the place.

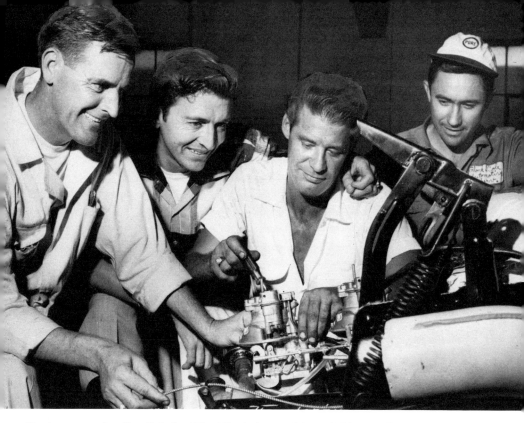

Racing was a family affair for Tim Flock (second from left). *His brother Bob* (left) *won four Grand National races before restricting his activities as his little brother's crew chief. Mechanics Emmett Mitchell* (center) *and Cecil Cole also worked on Tim Flock's stock cars.*

"I wanted to meet Baker so I went over to him after the race. I walked right up and said, 'Hey, aren't you Buck Baker?' He said, 'Yeah, why?' " Morris laughs. "He thought I was a spectator wanting to cause him some trouble. I noticed he had a cast on his hand and found out later he'd been in a fight after a race at the Charlotte fairgrounds. Racing people used to swing first and ask for conversation later back in those days."

Morris soon joined Baker as a mechanic. "I sort of considered myself the team manager," says Morris with a chuckle. "I did about everything there was to do. I was the gopher. Go for this and go for that." When Baker went to work for Kiekhaefer as a driver of one of the Chryslers, Chic Morris was included in the arrangement.

Morris recalls Kiekhaefer as the most successful individual sponsor in the history of stock car racing. "There have been countless stories told on Kiekhaefer," says Morris, "some true, some false. The best thing about him is he was a perfectionist. I guess Buck Baker placed in the top three in 50 per cent or more of the races we ran for him in that one season. Kiekhaefer has the reputation of being a heartless man, but his heart was bigger when he was involved in racing than for all of his factories put together. Racing was a plaything for him, and when he decided to quit, he tried to look after the people who were working for him. He had won everything there was to win and it was no longer fun for him. He called in most of his employees and asked if they'd like to work for his company, Kiekhaefer Mercury. He didn't bother to ask me. He told me, 'Morris, you're going into sales.' And I did."

Morris leaves no doubt in anyone's mind who he considers the greatest stock car driver of all time. His buddy, Buck Baker, of course. "Buck has always been dedicated to the sport," says Chic of Baker. "He could drive anything available in the early days and I guess he's won more races in more brands of cars—Fords, Oldsmobiles, Pontiacs, Chevrolets, Dodges, Chryslers and Hudsons—than any other driver."

Baker went further than that. He won a race in a Buick, a 1955 Grand National event at the Charlotte fairgrounds. And he beat Karl Kiekhaefer's Chrysler driven by Tim Flock while doing it. That was before Kiekhaefer figured he better hire the former Charlotte bus driver and 1953 winner of the Southern 500 at Darlington. Baker later won the Labor Day classic twice more. His three Southern 500 wins were all recorded in different makes of cars. He drove an Oldsmobile to victory in 1953, a Pontiac in 1960 and a Dodge in 1964. Baker took the Grand National championship in 1956 driving a Chrysler for Kiekhaefer as well as a Dodge. And he came back in 1957 to win the championship again in a Chevrolet. "They never made a car Buck Baker couldn't handle," says Chic Morris.

Perhaps the most stirring victory in Baker's career did not come in a Chrysler but in a Dodge. In 1964 many observers considered

Tim Flock stands beside his 1955 Chrysler before a Grand National race. The Chrysler, owned by Karl Kiekhaefer, carried the youngest of the racing Flocks to a record eighteen victories for one season. The record was not broken until Richard Petty won twenty-seven Grand National events during the 1967 season.

Baker at forty-four as over the hill when preparations began for the Southern 500 at Darlington. The old pro, whose son Buddy was beginning to make a name for himself, crawled into the cockpit of a Dodge prepared by veteran chief mechanic Ray Fox. Sportswriters gave him only a dark-horse chance of placing. After all, who should know better than Buck Baker that the Southern 500 is no test to be taken lightly by grandfathers still feeling their oats. It had been only four years, however, since Baker had driven the Pontiac prepared by Bud Moore into victory lane. It had been ten years since he drove the Oldsmobile into victory lane.

Experts agreed he had no chance of winning. He was too old for the grueling demands of the one-groove race track. His physical stamina could not match that of younger stars such as Plymouth's Richard Petty, Ford's Fred Lorenzen, Dodge's David Pearson and many others just beginning to carve places for themselves in the stock car racing sun. At forty-four years of age, the grandfather of a proud son's children, Buck Baker drove into the national limelight once again. For the third time, he won the rich Southern 500. And when all the hoopla was over, he walked away with a bouncy stride. Buck Baker wasn't tired at all. "He'll race forever," said his old friend Chic Morris.

Tim Flock, on the other hand, quit racing when he was reaching the pcak of what some would describe as a fantastic career. The winner of forty Grand National events had nothing else to prove. He had won the championship in 1952 driving a Hudson and repeated again in 1955 with the Kiekhaefer Chrysler. He drove no more after the 1956 season.

Tim's brother Fonty was also one of the drivers hired by Karl Kiekhaefer to drive the Chryslers during the 1955 and 1956 seasons. "Karl didn't miss hiring many of the good ones, the ones he thought wanted to win above everything else," says one observer of stock car racing for more than twenty years. "He wanted people who had a lot of pride. People who thought winning was the only thing in the world. He wanted people who didn't mind knocking a guy in the fender to see how that guy was going to act. Lots of times, I saw Kiekhaefer's drivers bang somebody in the fender when they knew they could run off and leave them."

Kiekhaefer's mark on the stock car racing world is in the record book. However, the man's business career is more of a mark. "When he told me I was going into sales," recalls Chic Morris, "he told me to find a place in Atlanta to build an office. I found one and he came down to look it over. When we got out to the site, he told me to call the Caterpillar people and find out the biggest piece of equipment they had to clear off some land. They told me what it was and asked if we wanted to come by and take a look at it. Karl told me to tell them to bring it on over. The guy hadn't been on the site two minutes before Mr. Kiekhaefer had that big old piece of equipment knocking down trees and clearing off land. The salesman didn't know what to think. Kiekhaefer asked him what he wanted for the bulldozer. The guy told him and Kiekhaefer wrote him a check."

When Kiekhaefer checked out of racing following the 1956 season, Chrysler checked out with him. A Chrysler Grand National machine won only one race after that. Buck Baker captured a 100-miler in 1961 driving a beat-up old Chrysler only Baker could have driven in such a competitive manner.

9 THE MERCURY DRIVERS

→

Darel Dieringer grew up around Indianapolis. Cut his racing teeth on tires, you might say. The Indiana native took on any job he could to learn what it took to become a race driver. He worked as a tire changer. He worked as a mechanic. Wherever the racing wheels rolled, Darel Dieringer was there. Stock cars. Midget cars. Indianapolis cars. It didn't matter to the Hoosier youngster. He knew what he wanted and was willing to work for the chance.

It didn't take Dieringer too many years to convince himself he was going to be a race driver. Once he crawled into the cockpit of a stock car, it didn't take him long to convince others either. Dieringer, besides boyhood dreams of becoming a race driver, had one other burning desire. He wanted to win the Southern 500 at

Darlington, he wanted to drive into victory lane on Labor Day after conquering the toughtest track and one of the most prestigious stock car races.

In the late 1950s executives of the Mercury Division of Ford Motor Company had long since given up hope of winning major stock car racing events. Corporate brother Ford seemed to get the best mechanics and drivers. Mercury's styling over the years did nothing to enhance hopes of racing superiority. By 1960 the Mercury had become known in stock car circles as a sled. The term was not exactly flattering, but neither were the past performance records of Mercury stock cars.

Mercurys driven by Bill Blair and Lloyd Moore captured a pair of insignificant Grand National events in 1950. Mike Burke and Bob Norton won a pair of Grand Nationals on the west coast the following year. Billie Myers, an extremely popular Grand National driver from Winston-Salem, North Carolina, and a tremendous competitor, won a couple of races driving a Mercury in 1956. However, Mercury was hurting for national prestige in the speed-and-horsepower department by the end of the 1960 season. Likable Bill Stroppe launched a campaign for a couple of seasons with a fleet of Mercury machines, but Stroppe's effort fell short.

Veteran car builder Bud Moore of Spartanburg, South Carolina, was given the task of making Mercury competitive in 1964. Moore, with Little Joe Weatherly at the wheel, was the first chief mechanic to achieve any degree of success with the machine. Billy Wade, a native Texan, swept the Grand National northern tour in a Moore-prepared Mercury. Wade later died testing the machine, in a crash at Daytona International Speedway.

Dieringer, who was among NASCAR's leading drivers and had driven a Mercury prepared by Stroppe, signed on with Moore for the latter portion of the 1965 season. He came within an eyelash in 1964 of fulfilling his lifelong dream at Darlington. Dieringer had the Mercury well ahead of the pack 50 miles from the finish. A fire in the car's differential sent him into the pits for the day. He still finished third. The hard-driving Dieringer refused to give up. The 1964 Southern 500 put the taste of roses in his mouth. "I knew

LEFT: *Cale Yarborough, the former Timmonsville, South Carolina, high school football star, did his best running in a Mercury on the NASCAR stock car circuit. He's also proven his driving skill in championship cars at Indianapolis. But he's most at home running flat-out with the "good ole boys." And Yarborough was one of the drivers most responsible for Mercury's glory days on the stock car tracks.* RIGHT: *LeeRoy Yarbrough wasn't even old enough to own a driver's license when he first started fooling around with racing in Jacksonville, Florida. LeeRoy went from dragging on dirt roads on the outskirts of town to "legal" dirt tracks to superspeedways to Indianapolis. But his name became a household word in stock car racing as part of Mercury's team, which dominated the superspeedways for several seasons. Yarbrough's biggest year was 1969 when he won at Daytona, Atlanta, Darlington and Charlotte and made over $180,000 in purse money.*

after that race I could win the Southern 500," he said. "I knew it was possible."

In 1966 Dieringer's dream came true. He wheeled the Moore-prepared Mercury home ahead of Richard Petty and David Pearson to win the Southern 500. For Dieringer, it was the happiest day of his life. For Moore, it was his second trip to victory lane for the Labor Day classic. He had prepared the Pontiac driven to victory by old pro Buck Baker in 1960.

While the Moore Mercurys were trying to break the winning ice for Ford's corporate brother, Grand National fans constantly scanned the result sheets to see the finish position of Curtis (Crawfish) Crider, a longtime Mercury driver from Charleston, South Carolina. Crider was one of few regulars on the Grand National circuit who drove a Mercury year after year. He never won a race, but Crider impressed fans with his dogged determination to finish every event.

Just as Mercury's body style and bulky size hurt its competitive chances during the early days of Grand National races, a change in styling during the late Sixties boosted the machine into the ranks of major winners. And a pair of South Carolinians helped put it there. Cale Yarborough and LeeRoy Yarbrough pinned Mercury on the racing map for good. For the first time in stock car history, Mercury's body style was better suited for racing than Ford's as the 1968 Grand National season neared.

Cale Yarborough, "the one with the extra *o* in his name," was the scourge of the superspeedways. Driving a Mercury prepared by one of stock car racing's best-known teams, Cale won both the Daytona 500 and Firecracker 400 at Daytona, the Southern 500 at Darlington and the Atlanta 500 at Atlanta International Raceway. When Cale wasn't winning, LeeRoy was. But LeeRoy's big year was 1969 when he grabbed the Daytona 500 and Firecracker 400, Darlington's Southern 500 and Rebel 400, Atlanta's Dixie 500, the World 600 at Charlotte Motor Speedway and the Carolina 500 at North Carolina Motor Speedway.

Race fans, for three seasons, heard little or saw little of anyone except the two young South Carolina drivers. Things were not always so good for Cale and LeeRoy, however. In fact, if anyone ever deserved to be big winners in Grand National competition, Cale Yarborough and LeeRoy Yarbrough did. Joe Whitlock, a longtime friend of Cale's, watched his buddy bounce off the walls in inferior equipment for almost five years before he ever landed a decent ride.

"I remember Cale's first steady deal," says Whitlock, now a

LeeRoy Yarbrough's ready to roll. A few years ago he teamed with Cale Yarborough (the one with the extra o in his name) and they dominated the NASCAR circuit. LeeRoy now lives in Columbia, South Carolina, and still drives the dirt tracks around that area from time to time, although he's taken home purse money from almost every major superspeedway race.

member of the Daytona International Speedway publicity staff. "It was a couple of days after the July Fourth race down here in 1963. Cale and his wife, Betty Jo, drove up to Myrtle Beach, South Carolina, for a race. I went too. Cale's aunt or cousin or somebody had a cottage at the beach and we stayed there for a couple of days. Cale was taking over Herman Beam's 1963 Ford. His first race in the car was the 100-miler at the old half-mile Myrtle Beach track.

"They didn't have a pit crew. Just Herman and Cale. I was drafted. I had to borrow a water can and some gas and a rag to wipe the mud off the windshield. I don't even remember how he finished, but it wasn't very good." Cale, driving the Ford most fans knew belonged to one of the slowest drivers on the circuit (Beam was called "The Turtle"), opened some eyes. He led some races in the car.

But the native of Timmonsville, South Carolina, just a few miles down the road from Darlington, had to supplement his racing income with various trades he had learned over the years. He logged and he farmed and he raised turkeys. "I lost my shirt in the turkey business," he says. All the while, Cale Yarborough looked for the ride that would take him to the front of stock car racing's pack.

Yarborough was a born athlete. Strong and stocky, he played semi-pro football for a couple of seasons. He also had more than enough guts. His idea of fun was catching water moccasins or wrestling alligators or free-falling out of an airplane. He used to laugh when he told the story of how he missed the entire Atlantic Ocean during a skydiving exhibition. "It was at the Beaufort, South Carolina, Water Festival," Cale recalls. "I got caught in a big draft while we were jumping out over the bay where the festival was being held. I landed on a bank downtown. People kidded me about missing the whole ocean."

Cale kept searching for the ride to make him a contender. "I remember every spring and summer," says Whitlock, "Cale would drop by the house on the way to a race, and he'd have cucumbers and corn and fresh tomatoes and farm stuff like that. We'd talk about racing, and then he'd go somewhere and drive the fenders off whatever he could get his hands on."

Cale signed on to drive a Ford in the 1965 Southern 500. It was his best ride to date. The car was built by Banjo Matthews, the former driver turned car owner. But what started out as Yarborough's most promising day wound up in near-disaster. Whitlock, who was in the Darlington press box, describes Yarborough's worst accident and one of the most spectacular in Darlington's long history.

"Cale tangled with Sam McQuagg as they went into the first turn right underneath the press box," says Whitlock. "All of a sudden, Cale's car is sailing over the fence like an airplane. It just went into orbit. I remember I had a sick feeling in my stomach as I ran down to where his car had sailed over the fence. The car was crumpled all up, and steam was rising in a mist from the wreckage.

A. J. Foyt doesn't race stock cars very often, but when he does—especially at the wheel of a top car—he's tough to beat. Foyt has driven Wood brothers-owned Mercurys to victory at Atlanta, Daytona and Ontario superspeedways. The Wood brothers are not only top car owners and builders, but are generally conceded to be the world's fastest pit crew.

And sitting on the ground beside the car, cussin' like a fool and kicking the ground, was Cale, his eyes big as half-dollars. He forced a smile and said, 'Aw, hell. I'm all right.' "

It was the first time Yarborough had gone over a fence in a car and hopefully his last, but NASCAR chief steward Johnny Bruner could remember the stocky little native being forced behind Darlington's fence long before that day in 1965. "I remember running him out of the pits when he was just a teen-ager," says Bruner. "He talked somebody into letting him drive for them. We'd throw him out because he was underage, and a few minutes later, somebody would come and tell me he was back in again.

"I caught him during a pit stop one Labor Day. We had told him he couldn't drive. He must not have been but fifteen or sixteen years old then. The first pit stop, Cale sneaked into somebody's car. I figured then he would someday be a great race driver. Anybody wanting to drive as much as he did when he was a kid was bound to make it."

Yarborough's ambition became reality beginning with the 1967 season when he won two of sixteen races he entered on the Grand National circuit. The South Carolinian also escaped from another spectacular accident unharmed. Whitlock remembers that 1966 accident at Indianapolis also. It was Yarborough's first year at the famed old brickyard and the race had just begun. The flag had just been dropped. "There was nine hundred million dollars' worth of equipment all piled up and the race hadn't even started good yet," says Whitlock, "and Cale was right in the middle of it. He told me later a piece of the debris split his helmet right down the middle and he isn't scared yet."

Cale won six major events in 1968 for $136,786 in prize money. The following season, he earned another $74,240, and in 1970, winning three more major events, Yarborough earned better than $100,000 for the second time in his career. Mercury fans fell in love with the gutsy little guy from Timmonsville, but their cheers were split between Cale and the other Yarbrough, the "one without the extra *o*."

LeeRoy's background was almost identical to that of Cale's, with the exception that LeeRoy had never jumped out of an airplane. Born and raised in Jacksonville, Florida, LeeRoy started the pursuit of a stock car racing career at an early age. Bumper tag was one of his specialities as a teen-ager. "Man, when I think about

Darel Dieringer, seen here working on his car in the garage area, had his biggest moment in racing while driving a Mercury—he won the 1966 Southern 500. Though Dieringer won seven Grand National races, this was his only major speedway victory. It was also the first major stock car race won by a Mercury.

some of the streets we used to go flying over outside of Jacksonville when I didn't have any better sense, it scares me just to think about it," says LeeRoy, whose first Grand National victory came in 1966 at the wheel of a Dodge.

Like Cale, LeeRoy proved the only thing keeping him out of Grand National victory lanes on a regular basis was proper equipment. Three times the Florida native who settled in Columbia, South Carolina, won the Permatex 300 at Daytona International Speedway for Late Model Sportsman cars.

It was not until 1969, however, that Yarbrough finally reaped the rewards of many trying years. He joined the Junior Johnson team in 1968, but a matter of split seconds kept him out of victory lane in the Daytona 500. He won Atlanta's Dixie 500 in 1968 and finished in the top five fifteen times of twenty-six races entered. He won $86,654, the most money he had made in eight long years on the Grand National trail. The following year, 1969, belonged to LeeRoy and his Junior Johnson Mercury. He started the season by winning the rich Daytona 500. He won major events on five super-speedways. He won $188,605 in prize money and was voted "Driver of the Year" by the National Motorsports Press Association.

Yarbrough, who patterned his driving style after that of Florida's most famous race driver, Fireball Roberts, won only one race in 1970, the National 500 at Charlotte, but hauled home another big chunk of $61,000 in prize money. He was sidelined most of the 1971 season by Rocky Mountain spotted fever but began a comeback after spending more than forty days in hospitals. At one stage during the illness, doctors did not expect LeeRoy to live. "They didn't exactly tell me I was going to die," he says. "They just told me to get all my personal things in order. When they tell you that, you don't sleep much at night."

He refused to give up and battled back despite several bouts with the illness that sent his temperature soaring above 104 degrees. By the beginning of the 1972 season Yarbrough's mind was back on winning. But it is doubtful Mercury fans will ever again enjoy winning streaks like those provided by LeeRoy and Cale during the 1968–69 seasons.

Former AAA champion Frank Mundy (left) stood the stock car racing world on its ears in 1951 when he set track records all over the south in a Studebaker V8 Commander. Car owner Perry Smith congratulates Mundy after the driving star won the pole position for the 1951 Southern 500 at Darlington.

Glenn (Fireball) Roberts thrilled Buick fans in Daytona with his daredevil driving. Roberts also almost won Darlington in a Buick (M-1) before a wheel broke, causing him to crash.

10 THE OTHER CARS

———————————————————————→

Fred Johnson, brother of the fabled stock car driver Junior, will never forget his last race. Fred can't help but laugh, for his career as a driver ended with class. Fred drove his last race in a Cadillac. He didn't run out of car, he ran out of tires. "We couldn't keep tires under it," he says with a laugh. "But it'd run. There wasn't any doubt about that."

Johnson's Cadillac lasted 231 laps of the 1955 Southern 500. "I wasn't tired or anything," Johnson says with a snicker, "but the guys in the pits sure must have been—they had to change tires about every ten laps. Soon as they'd put new ones on, I'd be back in for some more a few laps later." Johnson's attempt at making a Cadillac competitive on the nation's stock car tracks was not the

Bob Burdick was among the drivers to put Thunderbirds at the head of the Grand National packs during the 1959 season.

first. It was perhaps the last, since the luxury car of today is simply too big and too heavy to compete with the smaller, lighter automobiles.

Rarely has a car been built that someone didn't race in Grand National competition at one time or another. Cadillacs, like that driven by Johnson. Thunderbirds, Buicks, Nash Ramblers, Lincolns, Packards, Studebakers, Kaisers, Henry-Js, DeSotos, you name it and somebody drove it. They didn't necessarily win, but they sure tried.

Fords, Plymouths, Chevrolets, Oldsmobiles, Dodges, Chryslers, Hudsons, Pontiacs and Mercurys have dominated the Grand National scene over the years. T-Birds, however, won six Grand National races in 1959. Lincolns won four Grand National events, Studebaker has three victories in the record book and Buick won a pair of races in 1955. Nash is also credited with a Grand National victory.

Don't get to scoffing at the idea of Cadillacs, Lincolns and the like zipping around the nation's speedways. The first race at Darlington, the 1950 Southern 500, was almost won by a Cadillac. "Red Byron finished third in the first race driving a Cadillac," recalls Darlington President Barney Wallace. "He had a chance to win, but tire troubles kept him in the pits too much. He was getting around the track a lot faster than Johnny Mantz, but Mantz didn't have to make nearly as many pit stops." The same car Byron drove to a third-place finish the first year was the lone Cadillac in the race the following year. Billy Carden drove the Caddie to a fourteenth-place finish.

"Just about every kind of car you can imagine was entered here the first few years," says Wallace. "Why, Frank Mundy's Studebaker was one of the hottest cars on the circuit in 1951. He qualified on the front row for the Southern 500." In a Studebaker? "Absolutely," recalls Mundy, who won a pair of Grand National races in the Studebaker. "It was one of the best-handling cars I ever drove," says the former AAA champion who later became one of Karl Kiekhaefer's Chrysler drivers. "The Studebaker had plenty of power and once we got the chassis worked out where I could get it through the corners, it was really something."

Mundy qualified the car for the pole position at Darlington in 1951 with an average speed of 84.65 miles an hour. He was driving for W. Perry Smith, a Studebaker dealer in Columbia, South Carolina. Smith took advantage of his stock car's performance. He ran ads saying, "Come in and see the spectacular new Studebaker Commander V8 . . . winner of the pole position for the 500-mile Darlington Labor Day Classic . . . winner of the 200-lap Grand National circuit race at Columbia Speedway . . . fastest qualifier for the 250-mile Detroit Anniversary Race."

Mundy set records at several other tracks during the 1951 season. He won a 150-lap event at Mobile, Alabama, to end the season. "You should have seen Mundy sling that Studebaker around the track," Alf Knight says with a big grin. "It had that old propeller-looking nose like a shark and that skinny tail end that looked like a hound dog's nose. But old Mundy sure 'nuff scored the hell out of everybody with that thing. He set new track records at just about all the short tracks."

Charlotte stock car fans had the privilege of seeing the only Nash victory in more than twenty years of Grand National competition. Curtis Turner drove a Nash Ambassador to first place in a

Red Byron, NASCAR's first Grand National champion, drove a Cadillac to a third-place finish at Darlington in 1951.

150-lap race over the old Charlotte Fairgrounds Speedway. Ironically, the race was held on April Fools' Day, but Turner and the Nash were no joke to Lee Petty, who finished second, and Marshall Teague, who was third.

Buick fans pride themselves on the fact that Fireball Roberts almost won the Southern 500 in 1955 driving their favorite car. The fabled Fireball earned the pole position for the race with a record speed of 110.682 miles an hour. He charged into a huge lead and was running away from the pack when a wheel collapsed, causing him to crash into the third-turn guard rail. Buicks won a pair of short-track Grand National races the same season.

A Lincoln driven by Jim Roper of Great Bend, Kansas, won two Grand National races in 1949. Tim Flock and Harold Kite won Grand National races in 1950 driving Lincolns.

The 1959 season was the year of the Thunderbirds. Joe Weatherly and Curtis Turner, along with Banjo Matthews, Tiger Tom Pistone, Bob Burdick and Elmo Langley, were contenders throughout the season. Pistone won a pair of races, as did Langley. Matthews, the man many people recall as the king of the modifieds, drove his T-Bird to the front of the field in virtually every race he entered, but luck never crawled into the cockpit with the Asheville, North Carolina, veteran and he failed to win. Jimmy Thompson and Tommy Irwin also tried their hands at the wheel of T-Birds.

Johnny Allen, the Grand National driver with nine lives, drove several races in a T-Bird. Allen, a native of Greenville, South Carolina, lived through three of stock car racing's most spectacular accidents. He crashed through the Darlington guard rail and knocked down the scorer's stand but escaped injury. His car caught on fire in the pits at Bristol and burned practically to the ground, but he was uninjured. His car ripped up more than 100 feet of guard rail in Atlanta before sailing down the 30-foot embankment. The engine in that wreck was ripped from the car and landed more than 150 feet away. Allen suffered only a broken nose.

Veteran driver Elmo Langley drove a Thunderbird into the lead of many Grand National races during the 1959 season.

Hard-luck Johnny Allen sat in every make car at one time or another during his Grand National career but his efforts usually wound up like this one. His Mercury burst into flames during the Southern 500 and Bobby Johns (72) just missed ramming into the burning machine. Allen survived numerous spectacular accidents.

Fans of the old Henry-J will find that Reino Tulonen of Fitchburg, Massachusetts, drove a Henry-J to a fortieth-place finish in the 1951 Southern 500. And Desoto buffs will quickly tell you Roy Hall of Atlanta drove one of their pride and joys to a forty-eighth-place finish in 1952. They will also tell you there were sixty-six cars in that race, meaning Hall's DeSoto did not finish last.

"I remember there were a few Willys that ran the circuit for a year or two," says Alf Knight. "Eventually, they got tore up. Folks got tired of them being in the way all the time so they just started knocking them off the track."

There was a Henry-J that people in Columbia, South Carolina, will never forget either. The former half-mile dirt track was what they called an "early" race track. Fans wanted to get to the track long before practice started. The biggest reason was a big, burly guy who ran a giant, diesel-powered water truck around the track at full speed. He stood on the gas through the corners as if he had the devil himself right on his bumper. An amateur driver turned up one night in a Henry-J. He never made the race. He drove onto the track while the water wagon was wetting down the turns. The water truck beat him around the oval two consecutive laps. He hooked the Henry-J to his tow car and headed back home. The record book doesn't show the race, but the water wagon, winner of that celebrated two-lap event, was a Mack.

11 THE TRACKS

→

"They ought to plow this place up and plant it in peanuts," Cale Yarborough said a few years ago at Darlington, South Carolina. The words landed like Pearl Harbor. Lifelong stock car fans were quick to counterattack. "The nerve of that young whippersnapper," cracked old-timers. "Why, if it hadn't been for Darlington, these youngsters of today would be racing for peanuts instead of telling somebody to plant them."

Darlington, you see, started it all. The "Granddaddy of Stock Car Racing" they call it. Drivers have called it worse in its day, much worse. The fact remains, Darlington was first. And, in the minds of many stock car fans today, still is. Twice a year, Confederate Memorial Day in the spring and Labor Day in the fall,

Darlington changes from a quiet rural community to a loud, bustling spot populated by transients.

At Darlington the cry is one of relief when each race is over. As Joe Weatherly once put it, "You don't get away with just beating the other cars and drivers here. You've got to whip this old track, too. She tries her damnedest to beat you. Just about the time you think you've got it mastered, you hit a slick spot that wasn't there the lap before and you're bouncing off the guard rail like a rubber ball." The 1⅜-mile track, with two turns high-banked and two relatively flat, was constructed in 1950. It was the brainstorm of Darlington native Harold Brasington, who returned from watching the 1949 Indianapolis "500" bursting with big dreams.

The race track was gradually shaped from land normally contoured with peanuts or corn or other southern crops. The first race offered $25,000 in prize money and attracted more than a hundred entries. "They brought them straight off the streets for that first race," says Floyd Lane, a member of Darlington's present board of directors. "They ran the same tires, same wheels, same everything practically. About the only thing they did different was strap the driver in the seat." The Southern 500 was to be Harold Brasington's answer to the Indianapolis "500" for "good ole boys" down South. The cars were to be the same as those driven to the local tobacco auctions or down the two-lane road for a chicken bog at Cousin Sue's Sunday after-meetin' dinner.

The first Southern 500 at Darlington attracted a gate-breaking crowd. "It seemed like a million people converged on us all at once," says raceway president Barney Wallace. "I imagine it was more like twenty-five thousand or so. We never could figure out just how many people came to that first race because they knocked down most of the gates and tore down the fences to get in." Seventy-five cars started the first Southern 500, but only twenty-six were running at the finish when Californian Johnny Mantz took the checkered flag in a black Plymouth coupe numbered 98.

For years Darlington was the lone track staging a lengthy stock car race for a healthy purse. Crowds steadily grew until more than 50,000 spectators jammed the concrete grandstands and dirt-

A Hudson Hornet leads the pack through the south turn at Daytona's old beach-and-road course. Prior to the days of the superspeedway circuit, this track was considered the most prestigious place to win other than Darlington. The cars ran south on U.S. A1-A, turned off through a sandy turn and roared back down the sandy beach.

packed infield at Darlington on Labor Day weekends.

Watching all of the Darlington big track success was William H. G. (Bill) France, president of the National Association for Stock Car Auto Racing, who had long envisioned a paved super-track in his adopted hometown of Daytona Beach, Florida. Having sanctioned Darlington's Southern 500 and Rebel 300 races each year from the track's very beginning, France was well aware of the potential such stock car races provided. He envisioned a massive 2½-mile, high-banked track in Daytona to replace the old beach-and-road course that served as home base for February's annual Florida Speed Weeks. In 1959 France's dream became a reality. Daytona International Speedway, with asphalt turns banked too steep to climb by foot, was ready for action.

Daytona was not only bigger and shaped differently from Darlington, it was also much faster. The tri-oval track harbored speeds well above 140 miles an hour, whereas Darlington, an egg-shaped oval, registered speeds some 20 miles an hour slower. Lee Petty won the first Daytona 500 Grand National stock car race in a photo finish with Midwesterner Johnny Beauchamp. Petty's average speed of 135.521 miles an hour stood the racing world on its ear and the superspeedway craze was born. Stock car racing, a ragtag also-ran for the public entertainment dollar during the Fifties, was on its way to becoming one of America's most popular spectator sports in the Sixties.

With Darlington and then Daytona providing 500-mile races for the kind of cars parked in garages throughout the country, other investors investigated possibilities of large, high-banked tracks in their areas. Charlotte Motor Speedway and Atlanta International Raceway broke ground. Backers of both based the two newest big tracks on viewing appeal. The idea was to build a track that offered the fan the same kind of view he received at the shorter tracks but to increase the drawing appeal by a tremendous increase in speed itself.

The superspeedway circuit of NASCAR was thus founded with Granddaddy Darlington, Big Daddy Daytona and first-generation offspring in the major metropolitan areas of Charlotte, North Carolina, and Atlanta, Georgia. Both Charlotte and Atlanta were 1½-mile, high-banked tracks, and both ventured into the stock car racing world underfinanced. The only difference between the two was the contour of the actual racing surfaces themselves. Charlotte was built as a scale-model version of Daytona, with a tri-oval shape, while Atlanta was constructed with long, sweeping turns and relatively short straightaways.

Charlotte Motor Speedway's first race was another first for Grand National cars. It was to be the world's longest stock car race, 600 miles. They named it the World 600 and Joe Lee Johnson, a Tennessee native, won the first race ever held at CMS in 1960. The track was barely finished in time for the opening event and the asphalt surface ripped apart under the pressure of the speeding machines. A court-appointed reorganization team was necessary to put the track on sound financial footing, but the track is today one of the nation's best, with North Carolina promoter Richard Howard guiding the corporation's future from his general manager's seat.

Popular Fireball Roberts won the first race ever held at Atlanta International Raceway in July of 1960. AIR, as it has come to be called, was also barely ready for the first race. "Hell, people were coming in race morning and having to wait for the construction crews to get out of their way before they could sit down," recalls AIR superintendent Alf Knight. "The asphalt was barely dry when they dropped the green flag for the start." Ernie Moore,

Knight's longtime sidekick and flagman of the first race at Atlanta International Raceway, recalls the first race with a laugh. However, he has to rub his neck every time anyone mentions it. "Ernie was busy as a bee the week before that first race like everybody else," says Knight. "He was scurrying around doing whatever needed to be done. He happened to be up at the NASCAR sign-in gate a few days before the race and these two race drivers he knew were begging NASCAR officials to let them enter. NASCAR didn't want to let them race, but old Ernie vouched for them. I never will forget those two."

Ernie Moore persuaded NASCAR to admit drivers Johnny Dollar and Tiger Tom Pistone to the inaugural event. As much as

The north turn of Daytona's old beach-and-road course was tricky since the cars slid through the corner on sand and came out on paved highway.

Darlington's infield has become famous over the years for its overnight guests. Fans come from all over the country to spend the Labor Day weekend at the nation's oldest superspeedway. Card games, cookouts and country music are the order of the weekend.

Moore liked the two, he lived to regret it. While Moore was flagging the race, Dollar's car lost a tie rod coming down the main straightaway. Pistone ran over the flying piece and it sailed up into the flagstand, hitting Moore in the neck. "I don't even remember what hit me," says Moore. "All I remember is Alf waking me up in the hospital late that night." The cut in Moore's neck required thirty-five stitches. "I got to the hospital late that night," recalls Knight. "Man, we were all tired after that first race. I walked into Ernie's hospital room and his wife Helen told me he was all right. So I woke him up and told him, 'Move over, Ernie, I'm just as tired as you are.'"

Atlanta suffered through several seasons of rainouts, plunging deeper and deeper into financial plight, but Nelson Weaver, an Alabama businessman who loved the sport, came to the rescue until his death. The track, located south of downtown Atlanta in Hampton, Georgia, was placed under court-appointed guidance in

1970 and will likely gain financial solvency such as that currently enjoyed by Charlotte, which underwent similar problems years ago.

Darlington, Daytona, Atlanta and Charlotte provided the basis for stock car racing's Grand Slam. Drivers compared winning events at each of the four superspeedways to golf's Grand Slam. However, the drivers soon had plenty of places to compete between superspeedway events. Martinsville Speedway in Virginia, for example, has provided fans with the best in short-track racing for years.

The Martinsville track is one of many half-mile courses on the Grand National circuit, but drivers and fans alike consider a pair of 250-mile events there each season as musts on the stock car

Darlington International Raceway, along with Pure Oil Company, founded the Pure-Darlington Record Club for the fastest qualifier in each make of car every Southern 500. The club is one of the most exclusive in auto racing and its members proudly wear the Record Club blazer, as in this 1962 group. Front row, left to right: *Richard Petty, Elmo Langley, Cotton Owens, Joe Weatherly, Rex White and Tiny Lund.* Back row: *Dick Joslin, Joe Eubanks, Glenn (Fireball) Roberts, Alfred (Speedy) Thompson, Marvin Panch and Bob Burdick.*

Richard King, first president of Atlanta International Raceway, breaks ground in 1959 with drivers Joe Weatherly (left) *and Curtis Turner looking on. A plan for the raceway is on the right in the picture.*

racing schedule. Martinsville president Clay Earles is one of the most popular management figures in stock car racing. The Martinsville facility is sculptured to the needs of the fans and is one of the most colorful tracks on the Grand National trail.

Other half-mile tracks that have long been a part of the NASCAR Grand National circuit are Bristol International Speedway in Bristol, Tennessee; Columbia Speedway in Columbia, South Carolina; Greenville-Pickens Speedway in Greenville, South Carolina; Hickory Speedway in Hickory, North Carolina, which operates under the capable leadership of former Grand National champion Ned Jarrett; Fairground Speedway in Nashville, Tennessee; Thompson Speedway in Thompson, Connecticut; North Wilkesboro Speedway in North Wilkesboro, North Carolina; Virginia State Fairgrounds Speedway in Richmond, Virginia, operated by personable Paul Sawyer, a longtime friend of Grand National drivers; and Smoky Mountain Raceway in Maryville, Tennessee.

Smaller tracks long staging Grand National events on a regular basis include Bowman-Gray Stadium in Winston-Salem, North Carolina; Islip Speedway in Islip, New York; New Asheville Speedway in Asheville, North Carolina; Old Dominion Speedway in Manassas, Virginia, and South Boston Speedway in South Boston, Virginia.

There have been many other short tracks staging Grand National stock car races over the years, but the middle of the 1960s brought about an ever-increasing number of bigger and better facilities. A scenic one-mile track was constructed in the sandhills section of North Carolina between Rockingham, Hamlet, Southern

Jack Smith's famous No. 47 Pontiac was the first stock car on the track at Atlanta International Raceway. Notice that the guard rail had not been installed.

Pines and Laurinburg in 1965. They called it, simply, the North Carolina Motor Speedway. The winner of the first 500-mile race there grabbed international headlines. None other than the old pro Curtis Turner chased the hurrying sundown across the finish line in that track's first major event.

Lawrence H. (Larry) LoPatin headed a group called American Raceways, Inc., which built two new tracks in 1968. LoPatin's group also merged with Atlanta International Raceway and Riverside International Raceway, the California road course that has served as the kickoff point for each new NASCAR Grand National season since 1963. Michigan International Speedway, about 60 miles from Detroit, and Texas International Speedway in Bryan College Station, Texas, are a pair of excellent two-mile superspeedways.

However, the biggest race track ever constructed was completed at Talladega, Alabama, in 1969, once again the brainchild of NASCAR president Bill France. Alabama International Motor Speedway is a 2.6-mile, high-banked track that is now the world's fastest superspeedway. Dodge driver Buddy Baker became the first race driver in history to top 200 miles an hour over a closed course when he toured the Talladega track at such astounding speed in 1970.

The first race at Talladega was a financial catastrophe since most of the Grand National drivers refused to compete under existing track conditions. Superstar Richard Petty and other leading drivers packed up their equipment and left the day before the scheduled first event. It was the first organized drivers' strike in NASCAR's history. The drivers did not feel the track was safe for competition due to unusually high tire wear. France felt it was. Though only Bobby Isaac of the name drivers chose to run in that inaugural Talladega event, the race was held, with young Richard Brickhouse the winner.

The following year, after the track surface was altered to meet the approval of leading Grand National stars, two Grand National 500-milers were held with newcomer Pete Hamilton, a former Sportsman champion, winning both in a Petty-prepared Plymouth.

168

Atlanta International Raceway packed in the crowds on clear days during its first years of operation but inclement weather forced many races to be postponed.

The Alabama track has since become one of the most competitive on the superspeedway circuit.

A one-mile track at Dover, Delaware, has also been added to the Grand National circuit for a pair of 500-mile races, and a 1½-mile track at Trenton, New Jersey, serves as a 300-mile stop-off for the stock car stars. There is no longer a race of less than 250 miles on the Grand National championship circuit.

The shorter tracks with limited spectator capacities no longer hold races for the Grand National championship division. "It is no longer feasible to hold Grand National events where less than 25,000 spectators can attend," says one veteran NASCAR official. "The purses have risen amazingly over the past ten years, and now it is almost impossible to get the top competitors for purses less than $100,000." Eventually, the Grand National circuit will probably consist of no events less than 400 miles with all purses topping the $100,000 mark.

The major events on the Grand National schedule, in the eyes of most competitors, consist of two races each season at each of the

Birmingham businessman Nelson Weaver rescued Atlanta International Raceway from financial despair and managed the track through some stormy years.

major speedways. The Daytona 500 and Firecracker 400 at Daytona, the Rebel 400 and Southern 500 at Darlington, the World 600 and National 500 at Charlotte, the Atlanta 500 and Dixie 500 at Atlanta, the Riverside 500 and a 400-miler at Riverside, the American 500 and Carolina 500 at North Carolina Motor Speedway in Rockingham, the Motor State 400 and Yankee 400 at Michigan International Speedway, and the Winston 500 and the Alabama 500 at Alabama International Motor Speedway in Talladega. A total of thirty-two races comprise the Grand National schedule in which points are awarded toward the Grand National championship.

Of all the tracks, drivers still consider Darlington the roughest on equipment. "You've got to stay on your tiptoes every second of every lap at Darlington," says veteran Bobby Isaac. "You can get into the wall awful easy at Darlington." That is because Darlington's turns are banked much less than those on most of the superspeedways.

Daytona and Talladega are referred to as "breath holders" by drivers. As one put it, "You're going so fast on those tracks, if anything happens to your car, all you can do is hold your breath and hope. There's not all that much you can do at two hundred miles an hour."

170

Charlotte and Atlanta are considered sidewinders. "Your car never has a chance to straighten out completely at Charlotte and Atlanta," says one veteran. "By the time you get out of one corner, you're going into another. Your car feels like it's always in a sideways drift—and it probably is."

The Rockingham track is considered another tough one on equipment. "Just about the time you get the engine wound out at the end of one of the straights," says Buddy Baker of the one-mile oval, "you've got to slow it down for the tight corners. It puts an awful lot of strain on the brakes as well as the engines."

Aerial view of the 2½-mile track at Daytona shows why it's referred to as a tri-oval—the front stretch, running from the fourth to the first turn, bulges out and has a pronounced curve in its middle. Built in 1959, Daytona International Speedway was the fastest closed course in the world until the Talladega speedway was constructed ten years later.

The Alabama International Motor Speedway at Talladega features the steepest banks in superspeedway history. The equivalent of five stories in height, the turns are banked 33 degrees. Initial problems with the track surface were quickly solved and Talladega now wears the mantle of the world's fastest closed course.

The two-mile tracks in Michigan and Texas are popular among the drivers. "They're wide and there's plenty of room to race," says Richard Petty. "You can run three and four abreast in the corners on those tracks without getting out of shape."

With grandstand capacities of more than 40,000 seats, modern rest rooms, full views of the action on the track, stock car drivers of today enjoy much better racing conditions than those who bounced and bumped through the cornfields and cow pastures of the early days of racing. Fans don't worry about heading home after an event caked in dirt and dust from the churning wheels. People dress up for major stock car races today, though there was a time when spectators wore something they could afford to get dirty while attending a race. Chalk it up to the modern facilities staging Grand National stock car events today throughout the United States. And chalk it up to the dream of Darlington's Harold Brasington, the man who wanted an Indy of the South. The dream's come true, from Darlington to Daytona and all through the South.

12 THE RULES

———————————————————————→

Grand National drivers, mechanics and car owners operate under rules established for the sport by the National Association for Stock Car Auto Racing. NASCAR is the "establishment" of Grand National competition. Like any governing body, participants and competitors do not always agree with existing rules. However, Grand National racing is just like any other professional sport. If you don't want to race by existing rules, you have to find some other place to race.

Basic rules for Grand National stock cars follow a format installed when NASCAR was formed in 1949. A car must be a current late-model passenger car, stock in appearance. Rules allow cars of the current year and two previous years to compete within certain guidelines. Makes are categorized into what NASCAR calls standard and intermediate sizes for Grand National competition. Wheelbases are restricted to a minimum of 115 inches. This rule is designed to keep participants from putting a big engine in a small car, which has been the trend in Modified racing for the past few years. Compact cars are not eligible for Grand National competition. Engine sizes are restricted to a maximum displacement of 430 cubic inches. Grand National cars must weigh a minimum of 3,800 pounds regardless of engine size. Cars are weighed when they are ready to race, which includes fuel, water and oil. Everything but the driver is included in the 3,800 pounds.

The rules are revised regularly, depending on how fast competitors learn to bend the existing ones. "As long as there are rules in stock car racing, someone is going to try to find a way to get around them," NASCAR technical inspectors are quick to point out.

Cars with approved engine sizes are required to use what NASCAR calls a carburetor restrictor plate. The plate serves to restrict the flow of air and fuel into the engine. In its simplest form, the use of the plate is designed to keep the cars from reaching astronomical speeds. It is also designed to maintain a reasonable closeness of competition as far as engine potential is concerned. The rule is designed to put the monkey on the driver's back. As one NASCAR official put it, "The ideal situation in every Grand National race would be to have every car exactly even from a mechanical standpoint. That way, the premium would be on the ability of the driver."

With the Detroit-based manufacturers no longer pumping millions of dollars into the sport annually, competition is back in the hands of the teams who want to work the hardest to achieve success. (Four-time champion Richard Petty made light of the fact that he became the first stock car driver to earn a million dollars in prize money because, as Petty put it, "I'm sure it took at least twice that much money to win the million dollars.")

Operating within the basic framework of the NASCAR rules, each competitor must explore every possible avenue for advantage.

Bill Gazaway, former chief technical inspector of the National Association for Stock Car Auto Racing, discusses Grand National rules with young driving star Pete Hamilton prior to a race.

For that reason, it has often been said that stock car racing is the only sport in which "cheating is a virtue." Surely you've heard the expression "Races aren't won on the race track. They're won in the garage area." Technical inspection of Grand National race cars is as thorough as a team of twelve NASCAR inspectors can make it. Engine sizes are checked. Carburetor plate sizes are checked. The car's body is checked by a template to make sure no illegal alterations, such as chopping the frame, have been made. The height of the car is measured according to NASCAR requirements. Still, there is constant disagreement over rules. Constant gripes.

Only the winner isn't cheating, they say.

"There probably isn't anything that hasn't been tried," says NASCAR's former chief technical inspector Bill Gazaway, who became Grand National competition director in 1972. "But we do our best to keep everyone right. The biggest thing is making sure we treat everyone the same way. They don't have an argument when that happens." One NASCAR technical inspector who used to be a driver says, "Inspection before a big race is like a game. They want to get away with anything they can. Sometimes they do. But I sure enjoy it when I catch somebody at something." NASCAR does not publicize those who are caught bending or breaking the rules. "We don't consider it necessary to embarrass anyone," says Gazaway. "Chances are everybody's been caught at one time or another."

Some of the things done by competitors over the years in Grand National competition to stretch the rules are humorous. Fred Lorenzen, one of the sport's all-time stars, was constantly teased

Former driving star Cotton Owens, who retired to become a car builder and chief mechanic, inspects spark plugs following a practice session. NASCAR mechanics go over their stock cars like skilled surgeons, looking for the least little sign of danger.

Highly respected Norris Friel, former NASCAR technical inspector, pokes his head into a crowd of drivers in garage area of Atlanta International Raceway. Friel, who died in 1964 after a lengthy illness, was highly respected by competitors for his sense of fair play. Friel enjoyed an occasional joke with drivers. About the picture above, he said that with so many drivers in a crowd, there was bound to be something "fishy going on." Looking on are, left to right: *Billy Wade of Houston, Texas; Tiny Lund of Cross, South Carolina; David Pearson of Spartanburg, South Carolina; Friel; Fred Lorenzen of Elmhurst, Illinois; and Jim Paschal of High Point, North Carolina.*

by other drivers about running an oversized gas tank. Robert E. (Bob) Colvin, the witty promoter who served as president of Darlington International Raceway until his death from a heart attack in 1967, had Lorenzen biting his nails one year during practice for the Southern 500.

Norris Friel, then chief technical inspector, had brought several confiscated items to Colvin to put in the Joe Weatherly Stock Car Museum as displays. The items were illegal apparatus picked up over the years by Friel and his inspectors. Friel brought along such pieces as aluminum hoods and fenders, lightweight bumpers and oversized gas tanks.

Colvin went over to the garage area and asked Lorenzen if he

Buddy Baker looks on while NASCAR inspectors weigh his Petty Engineering Dodge prior to a race. All cars must weigh no less than 3,800 pounds.

had seen his gas tank in the museum. When Lorenzen wanted to know what gas tank, Colvin told him it was one of those oversized tanks Friel had confiscated off his car. Lorenzen said he knew nothing about it. Colvin then told him it was over in the museum with a card that said something like: "This is an illegal, oversized gas tank taken off a car driven by Fred Lorenzen in Grand National competition." Lorenzen rushed over to the museum, but the card simply read: "This is an oversized gas tank." Colvin cackled for days. Lorenzen wouldn't speak to him.

Once aerodynamics became a dominant factor, competitors began looking for ways to lower their stock cars as much as possible. Rules emphasized that the cars must have a certain minimum clearance underneath. A measuring stick was used to slide under the car to check for this clearance. A common trick was to tape the shocks up while going through inspection or to block the suspension up high. Once on the track, vibration would knock the tape or blocks off and the car would automatically lower itself another inch or so. Competitors figured this was worth an extra hundredth of a second per lap. They don't waste any time telling you, either, what just a fraction of a second can mean on the track during qualifying or during a race.

Pit road observers at a Grand National race in Martinsville, Virginia, in 1964 couldn't help but snicker when Friel and mechanic Bud Moore became angry at each other because Moore's Mercury was too low. Friel told him to raise it. Moore said it wasn't too low. Friel, not one to argue, told the Spartanburg, South Carolina, chief mechanic to either raise the car or park it on his tow truck before the race started.

While Friel and Moore argued, Pops Eargle, a member of Moore's pit crew, winked at a couple of bystanders sitting on the pit wall. Eargle had found a couple of large flat rocks about the size of silver dollars, only an inch or so in thickness. He placed one of the smooth, flat rocks in back of each of the front wheels, and then he pushed the car up onto them. Moore and Friel were still arguing, with Friel mostly listening, when Eargle walked over and told Moore he had raised the car.

Friel took the measuring stick and poked it underneath the front end. He looked at Moore and said, "Why didn't you do that in the first place? I wouldn't have wasted all this time arguing." Satisfied, he left. Moore, wondering what Eargle had done to raise the car, could only scratch his head while Eargle and a couple of other Moore pit crew members casually leaned against the car and rolled it backward off the rocks. When Eargle kicked the rocks aside, Moore started giggling. Friel, no doubt, would have raged, had he known. Moore, however, could have pleaded innocence— he actually had nothing to do with it.

Controversy and squabbles seem to intensify when factories are involved with Grand National stock car racing. In recent years both Chrysler and Ford have caused leading drivers to sit out portions

New inner liners (a complete tire-in-a-tire) help prevent complete blowouts such as this and greatly reduce the number of severe accidents during races.

of the season while quibbling over rules with NASCAR officials. Chrysler drivers withdrew from NASCAR competition in 1965 when rules banned the use of the powerful Hemi engine. Ford's leading drivers did the same thing the following year for a period of time, once NASCAR again allowed the Chrysler Hemi to compete.

Important to drivers, mechanics and owners alike, safety regulations, such as allowing only steel-bodied cars to compete, are strictly enforced by NASCAR. The cars must also be equipped with heavy-duty suspension parts and a thick, solid roll cage must surround the driver in the cockpit. Grand National cars are also required to use fuel cells within the gas tanks to prevent explosions upon impact, and are required to use only racing tires which carry a built-in spare to prevent dangerous blowouts.

NASCAR polices the garage and pit areas to make sure no conduct detrimental to the sport occurs, and levies fines in cases of misconduct. The late Pat Purcell, NASCAR's executive manager, once said he fined driver Bobby Isaac so much in the early days of the North Carolina driver's career that "Isaac used to owe me money every week."

Cool tempers normally prevail on the Grand National circuit. The only time anyone gets mad is after losing. "And all the losers blame it on somebody," says one racing official of more than twenty years. "I've never seen a driver, chief mechanic or car owner who figured he lost a race himself. It's always somebody else's fault." And, of course, everybody else is always cheating.

"I remember a race one time when I knew everybody else was cheating and decided to cheat a little myself," says one well-known Grand National star. "I knew nobody would question me, because I knew they were cheating too. I put this big old engine in my car for a short-track race. Sure enough, NASCAR didn't check the engine sizes before the race. I sat on the pole and I felt real good. Only everybody else was running a whole lot slower than I was. That worried me. Once the race started, I got about a half lap ahead before I knew it. By the first pit stop I had lapped the field, so I slowed down. I was still running faster slowed down than

One of the latest developments in racing car safety is a nylon mesh screen which keeps a driver's head and arms inside the car in case of a violent flip or series of roll-overs. The screen unhooks at the bottom to allow the driver to get in and out of the car.

they were flat out, and pretty soon I had a full lap and a half on the field.

"I got to thinking it would be terrible if I won the race and somebody protested and they caught me cheating, so I pulled into my pits about thirty laps from the finish. My chief mechanic didn't know what in the world I was doing. I told him I didn't want to win the race and be caught cheating, so I just sat there and we played like we were doing something under the hood for about three laps. When I went back on the track, there were two cars ahead of me with only ten laps to go. I figured nobody would protest if I finished third, but damned if the two cars in front of me didn't blow and I ended up winning the race anyhow.

"I didn't know whether anybody would protest or not. They didn't, but the guy that finished second got an extra $200 out of me. He came over and told me he knew I was cheating but really didn't want to protest. He said he'd just forget about it for $200 and I gave it to him. On the way home that night I got to thinking how crazy I was for giving him that money. The reason he didn't want to protest was because he was probably cheating, too, and didn't want them looking at his engine." The driver laughed. "Live and learn. You can't be a race driver if all you can do is drive." Which is where the rules come in.

TOTAL VICTORIES BY MAKE OF CAR

(1949-1971) ⟶

FORD	269
PLYMOUTH	162
CHEVROLET	114
DODGE	111
OLDSMOBILE	87
HUDSON	79
PONTIAC	69
CHRYSLER	59
MERCURY	44
T-BIRD	6
LINCOLN	4
STUDEBAKER	3
BUICK	2
NASH	1

DRIVER VICTORIES FOR
GRAND NATIONAL STOCK CARS

(1949-1971) ⟶

Richard Petty	140	Fred Lorenzen	26
David Pearson	60	Jim Paschal	25
Lee Petty	54	Joe Weatherly	24
Ned Jarrett	50	Jack Smith	21
Junior Johnson	50	Fonty Flock	19
Herb Thomas	49	Speedy Thompson	19
Buck Baker	46	Curtis Turner	17
Tim Flock	40	Marvin Panch	17
Bobby Isaac	36	Dick Hutcherson	14
Fireball Roberts	32	Cale Yarborough	14
Bobby Allison	29	LeeRoy Yarbrough	14
Rex White	26	Dick Rathmann	13

Paul Goldsmith	9	Billy Wade	4
Cotton Owens	9	Bob Flock	4
Marshall Teague	7	Tiny Lund	3
Bob Welborn	7	Dick Linder	3
Jim Reed	7	Frank Mundy	3
Darel Dieringer	7	Bill Blair	3
Donnie Allison	6	Gwyn Staley	3
Ralph Moody	5	Red Byron	2
Dan Gurney	5	Gober Sosebee	2
A. J. Foyt	5	Danny Letner	2
Buddy Baker	4	Bill Myers	2
Charlie Glotzbach	4	Parnelli Jones	2
Pete Hamilton	4	Marvin Porter	2
Hershell McGriff	4	Johnny Beauchamp	2
Lloyd Dane	4	Tom Pistone	2
Eddie Pagan	4	Bobby Johns	2
Eddie Gray	4	Emanuel Zervakis	2
Glen Wood	4	Jim Pardue	2
Nelson Stacy	4	Elmo Langley	2

Other drivers winning one Grand National race: Jim Roper; June Cleveland; Jack White; Harold Kite; Bill Rexford; Johnny Mantz; Leon Sales; Lloyd Moore; Lou Figaro; Jimmy Floria; Tommy Thompson; Neil Cole; Mike Burke; Danny Weinberg; Bob Norton; Buddy Shuman; Dick Passwater; Al Keller; John Soares; Chuck Stevenson; Johnny Kieper; Royce Hagerty; Art Watts; Bill Amick; Danny Graves; Frankie Schneider; Shorty Rollins; Joe Eubanks; John Rostek; Joe Lee Johnson; Jim Cook; Bob Burdick; Johnny Allen; Larry Frank; John Rutherford; Wendell Scott; Sam McQuagg; Paul Lewis; Earl Balmer; Jim Hurtubise; Ray Elder; Benny Parsons; Mario Andretti; James Hylton; Richard Brickhouse.

INDEX